THREE CHAPTERS
ON THE
NATURE OF MIND

MACMILLAN AND CO., Limited
LONDON · BOMBAY · CALCUTTA · MADRAS
MELBOURNE

THE MACMILLAN COMPANY
NEW YORK · BOSTON · CHICAGO
DALLAS · SAN FRANCISCO

THE MACMILLAN CO. OF CANADA, Ltd.
TORONTO

THREE CHAPTERS

ON THE

NATURE OF MIND

BY THE LATE

BERNARD BOSANQUET
D.C.L., LL.D.
FELLOW OF THE BRITISH ACADEMY

MACMILLAN AND CO., LIMITED
ST. MARTIN'S STREET, LONDON
1923

KRAUS REPRINT CO.
New York
1968

COPYRIGHT

L.C. Catalog Card Number A23-2356.

Reprinted with the permission of the original publisher
KRAUS REPRINT CO.
A U.S. Division of Kraus-Thomson Organization Limited

Printed in U.S.A.

PREFATORY NOTE

THE following chapters on the Nature of Mind were written as introductory to a longer work upon which my husband was engaged up to the time of his last illness. He desired that they should be published as they stand in case he should not live to finish the book. I have given them the name of "The Nature of Mind," because that is how he described the subject to me when he began writing; but the complete work was to have been much more comprehensive in its scope, and it was his intention that it should be in the main constructive rather than critical. For this he had suggested provisionally and had pencilled on the MS. the title "Thought, Consciousness, Universe." It seemed better to retain the shorter title for these preliminary chapters.

HELEN BOSANQUET.

CONTENTS

CHAPTER I

WHAT A MIND IS FOR THE BIOGRAPHER
OR THE NOVELIST

BEFORE considering any philosophical analysis of the human mind it seems worth while to try and set down what sort of thing we take it to be when we describe it for its own interest in a biography or a romance.

We think of it, I suppose, in the first instance as a consciousness. We describe its contents and its purposes, and I think we read back its powers into our interpretation of what it is, though we know of course that the powers are largely latent, but in what way, we are not prepared to explain.

1. The simplest case, in which conscious-

1   B

ness is treated almost like a receptacle, is that of knowledge. Great " stores " of knowledge are not indeed what the highest judgment holds most admirable. We remember Jowett's description of a certain writer as " a learned man in the worst sense of the word." But to possess such stores is a character which we readily attribute to the mind. We hear it of the old man in the *Odyssey*, who " knew ten thousand things." A journalist attributed to Bishop Thirlwall " the almost boundless knowledge, before which all history lies like an open book." We are brought to recognise here a risk of absurdity by Anstey's caricature of the Hyde Park orator, " I am speakin' now with all 'istry vivid to my reckerlection "; and we have again the popular wonder at it in Goldsmith's village :

> And still they gazed, and still the wonder grew
> That one small head could carry all he knew.

This extent of possession is not, we said, in itself a very admirable endowment. But it has affinity with very great things, and is almost necessary, as the basis of many such. " The great folio editions of mankind," Walter Scott, for example, says William James, " almost always show this physiological retentiveness." The biographer or novelist would not call it by that name, but he means the same thing. His hero carries about, as it were inside him, an immense array of things, a great proportion of the world, compared with the belongings of common men.

If we are apt to overvalue sheer knowledge, and also, neglecting its latency, to think of it as " all vivid to " the possessor's " recollection," it is also possible to undervalue it. The hero-worshipper of a man whose knowledge is of wide range and whose memory is extraordinary has a good deal of justification. The phrase " to learn —to know—by heart," whatever may have been its origin, has a genuine meaning. It ought, one would think, to be just opposed to knowing by rote, with which it is usually confounded. To know by heart must be to know because we care,

and have given our best interest and attention. To know by rote should mean, I
suppose, to know by unintelligent habit
or repetition. To know the names of the
Derby winners for fifty years back is not
a very admirable accomplishment; but,
unless acquired for a wager, it at least
indicates an interest in the turf. But to
know " by heart " a large range of good
poetry, or the statistics of commerce or of
industry, or the manners, language, and
localities of a country-side (for the phrase
may be used in this significance also) is
no mean evidence of wide interests and
unselfish temper.

Thus the biographer or novelist, if he
argues that a mind with ample contents
is a large or ample mind, is not *prima facie*
wrong. He does not refine upon the distinction between the mind and its objects.
If a man knows the *Agamemnon* of
Aeschylus by heart, his mind, it would
seem, is more of a mind by that knowledge. He may have learned it for a bet
or for a prize, and his possession of it may

therefore be highly unintelligent. But after all, he has it ; he has it in its own proper form and nature of words and verses. It is difficult to suppose that such an object, thus made one with the texture and tissue of his mind, so that, for example, it can hardly fail to be a frequent source of associative cross references to other noble poetry—it is difficult to suppose that such an object so " known by heart " has not become one with the very nature and structure of the mind. The poem is not there if you have the words only; that is true. But again, you cannot have the poem unless you have the words, and the words exactly. It is not likely that having these you should fail to absorb something of their qualities into your own being. Lord Cockburn indeed tells a story of a Scottish colleague who was understood to pass two hours in the early morning, every day of his life, in studying Herodotus ; but no appearance of any mental result from the process, of any sort or kind, was ever detected in him by any friend or acquaint-

ance ; and it came to be believed that so
far as intellectual profit was concerned he
might as well during those hours have been
asleep and snoring. But this seems an
extreme case, to be matched, no doubt,
on occasion, by those who study something
a little out of the way merely to say they
have done it.[1] They could surely not be
said with truth to know the thing " by
heart." It is difficult to believe that in
the main it is possible for objects to be
embodied, in their own proper form of
ordered words, in the very life and structure of the mind, without in some degree
permeating its texture and tissue. I will
confess that in the early stages of the discussion concerning mind and its objects,
this case of things " known by heart "
presented to me a considerable difficulty
in thinking of those objects as other than
psychical in their nature, at least in one
aspect. But I am not just now discussing

[1] " If that is all, you could say it just as well without having
done it," as was observed to some one who gave this reason
for going down a coal mine.

philosophy or psychology.   All I am saying
is that there is much *prima facie* justification for taking great knowledge as connected with greatness of mind.   George
Eliot was, I think, a little malicious in
portraying Mr. Casaubon, and the bias of
a school is traceable in her picture.   Both
to her, and to the connection of knowledge
and disposition which she is caricaturing,
one might apply the saying, " Love speaks
with better knowledge, and knowledge with
clearer love."

Further, as we saw, words are not the
only things that we can " know by heart."
I am not competent to argue upon the
case of music, or to say in what a musical
memory consists.   But it is clear, I suppose, that the well-skilled lover of music
possesses within himself the essential elements of an immense region or fabric of
ordered sound.   I am not supposing the
biographer to trouble himself about such
distinctions as that of soul or subject as
against mind in general.   I shall say a
word on this point below.   But if we did

wish to talk of what we value most in a man's inner being, and if we attach importance to such an expression as that the iron has entered into his soul, must we not admit also that there is a sense in which music finds a place there ?

From this point we may leave the analogy to extend itself. To know by heart a country, a history, a people, a friend, or a wife means something ever further from inclusion of them *in propria persona*, in a sort of container, as we seem to include the sentences we could write down. But still our experience enlarges, as we say, our mind; and James's expression " the folio editions of mankind " suggests what the biographer attempts to indicate in describing, say, Goethe or Walter Scott.

A brief word of discrimination, on which we must not stay to argue, may be helpful here.

We said that the biographer has his eye fixed mostly on his hero's consciousness, or on his hero as a consciousness. This point of view, out of its *naïveté*, might develop well or ill. It would develop ill if it led us to insist on consciousness as the receptacle or container, in which all the contents of a mind can be surveyed like the furniture of a room or the picture which is a panorama. It would, nevertheless, in my judgment develop well if it caused us to consider the mind, though far from wholly present at any moment in or to explicit consciousness, yet as growing by what it feeds on, and having its unity rather in the interrelation and interdependence of its constituents than in any conceivably separable unifying principle brought in from " out of doors."

The biographer, we may say, describes his hero's consciousness, because it is easier to describe a concentrated essence, into which all outgoings are read back and interpreted, than to frame a unitary picture by depicting the outgoings themselves in this form of succession, the common ground of which is matter of inference. Of course he narrates actions at length, but he feels that he gets nearest to what the man is when he tells you what he thinks and loves and purposes. So he leans to treating the mind as a receptacle, and we meet with such extravagances as the idea that if you could get at Shakespeare himself, as he was in his own mind, you would find there a sort of reservoir, a superfluity, greater and richer than all his works, like the imaginary mass or store of a nation's wealth, which the ignorant suppose to be lying ready for distribution. It is well to remind ourselves, as against such a superstition, that if, so to speak, we could get at the explicit being of a creative or accumulative mind at any limited moment, we might find little or nothing there. We might use the extreme analogy of a pencil point, which by traversing a complex series of movements can leave behind it a splendid and intricate pattern, but has never had in it at any instant any appreciable portion of the design. The works, we might so apply our fancy, are what the man succeeded, throughout hard and confusing conditions, in grasping and rescuing from chaos, one by one and piece by piece, into their several pure and splendid forms. But they never were all there in him as in a gallery or library ; they were severally and progressively wrought out of the ore and dross which the sequences of experience forced upon him within and without; and in this sense it is in the works we must look for the fulness of the man, not in the man for a greater fulness than that of the works.   This is to prepare us for the relative truth of the evacuating interpretation, for which mind is mainly a complex of habits and behaviours not necessarily conscious at all.   But here, in speaking of the naïve romancer or biographer, we maintain that he is not practically very far wrong when he admires a comprehensive consciousness as indicating a great mind.

The biographer will ascribe to his hero abstruse and lofty thoughts. Here again what he probably has in mind is a character of the man's consciousness. And here again his meaning may very well be right. What he notices is that his hero's attention is occupied with assertions and suppositions which treat of properties unnoticed by the everyday observer of the outer world or of the world of conduct. They may be such properties of objects as are treated of by science or by philosophy; and their nature will be to be very far-reaching; that is, to concern for identical reasons a very great number of objects which for our everyday experience have isolated and individual interests. Thus Leibniz, for example, or Heine again, looks at our ordinary world from an unusual point of view, and says things about it which are difficult to appreciate, and which are incompatible with our customary attitude. And the biographer is right when he holds that their consciousness is preoccupied with matters which are not directly apprehended by sense-perception, and can only be brought to better understanding by careful reflective analysis. In this sense he calls his hero an abstruse thinker, and, as I have said, he is in the main within his right in doing so.

We shall, however, at a later stage, find a difficulty in precisely stating the relation of thought to consciousness. We all have the experience that even by attention we cannot altogether command the connections and sequences which we desire to obtain from thought. It is something which goes its own way, and has its own laws of operation, exhibiting itself rather in a control over our psychical life than in the contemplation of ideas or images which are the details presented as portions of that life itself. " The difficulty was so-and-so," one has heard a man say, whose organising ability was famous, " and it just occurred to me that Mr. X was the very man whose special capacity was needed to deal with it." " It just occurred to me," that is, the situation developed itself in his mind, proved fertile, continued itself in a relevant and appropriate manner. The right connections were awakened, and proceeded to the adequate result. This way of speaking will often be found in any one who is at once highly gifted and modest, or, at any rate, accurate and careful, in his phraseology. It is noticeably the attitude of creative thought and imagination. "It came to me." "At last I saw light." "The problem took a new shape in my thoughts." "That suggestion transformed the whole aspect of the argument." Such language does not suggest that thought lies in contemplation of abstractions. It suggests something which is not like my looking at a picture, but more like the picture, according to some life and law of its own, readjusting and recreating its own particulars, and carrying them on to further phases.

It is not improbable that abstruse thinkers may themselves have been touched by the popular superstition which we believe to influence the ordinary hero-worshipper of mind. I cannot but think, though I speak as one very ignorant, that something of this kind is wrong with some forms of Indian philosophy. It strikes the outsider as contemplation at will, rather than as a necessary movement controlled by objective reality.

But this digression is anticipatory ; a mere warning. What I am urging here on the whole is in the opposite direction. Here, as in the realm of knowledge proper or accumulated experience, the biographer takes the consciousness as the man. If thought is not strictly explicit conscious-ness, yet it appears to consciousness by its operations and consequences in psychical life, and though nothing is harder than to gauge the quality of thought, yet the objects of attention tell us, on the whole, where the man's treasure is, and we con-clude that his heart will be there also.

2. The biographer, whether historical or through imagination, has a certain advantage of position over the analytic philosopher. In dealing with the unity of a man's being, this is very noticeable. Not having to theorise, but to describe, he takes his hero as he finds him ; and being to a certain extent a practical man, with a

picture to draw, he selects a standpoint,
though of course he is at liberty to vary
it, and looks at the effect of his object as
observed from that standpoint. He may
make, from a succession of standpoints, a
succession or variation of pictures. But
always, while he is looking, a unity is
presupposed so far as that there is something which can be portrayed. So that it
becomes a postulate that the man, as
represented, is one, though seen at any
moment and in any aspect, just by being
what he is. The delineator of his life and
mind may be embarrassed by conflicts of
aim and tendency within him or in different phases of his career. But they are
all there *prima facie* on the same level, all
claiming their part in the personality, all
to be taken on their respective merits as
deeper or more superficial belongings, with
no presumption that the man's being is
kept together more by one of them than by
another, unless by the superior intensity
or orderliness of one experience as compared with others.

These conditions place the portrayer of the hero, as I said, in a position of advantage compared with the analytic philosopher. He is not troubled—I do not remember ever to have seen such a thing hinted at in a " life " or a romance—with the question whether there is a " subject " or an " ego," or a " soul " which persists from birth to death, and perhaps beyond, and makes the essential oneness of the life and mind. The biographer, I said, is largely a practical man. He does not find this soul or ego anywhere observably at work, and therefore it would be useless to him if he believed in it ever so. For him the man must be what he can find in him ; and if he cannot find in him the material of a unity on the whole, why, he will hardly be tempted to write his life.

Thus, though or because he does not theorise, he is by his essential function placed in general on the side of what is at least an attractive and effective theory ; indeed, of all that kind of theory which looks for the mind's unity in the correla-

c

tions and interdependences of factors which come together in the mind or as the mind according to the laws of mental co-operation. He has, just because his function implies a naïvely descriptive purpose, three factors of sanity which are apt in reflective analysis to be held incompatible. Firstly, he has no hesitation in affirming the peculiar unity of consciousness as an obvious fact which needs no proof but merely indication. He simply depicts it as it presents itself before him. And, I think, it seems to him to be primarily and simply a unity of feeling. As a first approximation, without refining, one would connect it with pleasure and pain. We are a unity because our pain or pleasure affects our whole being at once, and our own being only. The oneness stands on its own merits through a quality which pervades and endures. So far, as we saw, he is on the side of those (I do not say he theoretically agrees with them, for probably the question has never occurred to him) who hold that " the unity of the self is indistinguishable from the unity of the complex of its experiences."[1] The complex of its experiences is just what he is interested in, and what he sets out to portray. He finds no use in " any ego, in any abstract subject, in any mind " as a centre within the complex. Nor, I think, does he find it necessary to connect the unity of consciousness with an external object any more than with an internal subject. The unity may be emphasised by this, but it is rooted in the primary feeling, and this runs throughout life. To repeat ; he relies on the unity, but ascribes it neither to subject nor to object—simply to what it is, a something analogous to a pleasurable or painful being.

Secondly, making use of no pure ego, he makes use of no act of a pure ego. This is another term of theoretical analysis which nothing suggests to him. The world of the man's experience is always changing ; reproducing its elements in modified forms, blending, inhibiting, reinforcing one

[1] Stout, *St. Andrews Papers*, p. 6.

experience by another. He portrays all this, I suppose, as he finds it. It is a world at work within the mind, or, if we like to say so, as the mind. And for the biographer, all it needs is to have its story told. Here comes an ingrained disposition, here an intellectual influence, here a temptation, here an ambition. Where is the man's mind ? Why surely, in all of these or none. They work themselves out, and this working is the act or acts. The acts, then, are not the same in every case and contrasted with their objects which differ. The mind is a number of things growing, interworking, progressing. All the acts are different ; they are the behaviour of experiences inspired by the laws of mind. But there is nothing to be called " the mind " of which there are empty acts exercised upon objects. At least, if there are, I am sure that the biographer cannot find them.

Thirdly, it seems to me that he is kept sane on the problem of unity and of consciousness, more particularly by attention

to an all - important fact, which the behaviourist, so far as I am informed about
him, neglects;   the fact of enjoyment.
Say, if you like, that knowledge is a habit
of words, and conduct a habit of movements — which ultimately, in the main,
include the case of words.   But the biographer will quite certainly tell you what
his hero enjoys and how he enjoys it,
extending no doubt his usage to the well-
known cases in which, for example, we
" enjoy " bad health.   I am not following
Prof. Alexander's example.   For him " enjoyment " implies a subject and its acts.
But I am not speaking about this.   What
I mean, mainly and fundamentally, is
the aesthetic aspect of experience.   And,
Heaven be praised, the dullest of us have
some kind of aesthetic experience every
day and, more or less, all day.   I do not
know what the behaviourist makes of this.
I must return to it when I speak of " the
Russell mind."   But thus far, surely, it is
plain and obvious.   No biographer worth
his salt will omit to tell you what makes

his hero happy or unhappy, what he appreciates, and to what he is indifferent. And here, so far as I see, you must think of the man's own consciousness—not what he says, nor what he does, but what—there is no other word so simple and so right—he enjoys.

This clinches the question of unity, and consciousness, and unity in consciousness. In enjoyment we are all these. Tell the biographer that his hero, when he is delighting in the sun or the sea, in a concert or a play, is not awake and alive to what he is experiencing, and he will treat you as insane. And if consciousness did no more for us than this, it would still be among the most precious of possessions. But, as we shall see below, it does very much more. In this, however, the biographer's grasp of it is certain and secure.

3. We have spoken of the biographer's interest in his hero's consciousness as revealed in knowledge. We spoke next of his attention to the oneness of the hero's being as obviously " enjoyed " in pleasur-

able and painful feeling, and in the aesthetic experience—the experience in which things make us happy or the reverse, straight-away, simply by being there, before our minds.

But there is something else that the biographer will be continually considering, and that is, his hero's desires, purposes, or ends.

And here once more, it seems to me, the biographer has a special advantage. Pursuing his descriptive purpose day by day, month by month, year by year, he will have to depict, no doubt, something which is not yet in existence as influencing and colouring throughout the mind with whose present he is concerned. It may be anything from our daily bread to an ambition which is to us a guiding star; but some sense of what is to come, and some forecast of its nature, however vague, he will certainly have to note as a central asset of any human mind. This is the aspect in which " ends," " desires," " pur-poses " are conscious. In it we " live," some more and some less, but all to some extent, " in the future." We have ideas of what we want, which may be much dispersed and fragmentary, or may, with more or less reflectiveness on our part, depend upon one another in a system. It has well been said that the real interest of a love-story, at least for the ordinary man, lies not so much, or at any rate not merely, in the love-romance by itself, as in the whole conflict and aspirations by which it develops the hero's nature and his powers, and exhibits him " piercing " (*percer*), " making his path " (*faire son trou*), and becoming a something in the world.[1]

Such a growth, including a whole section of a life, or perhaps a continuous life itself, is the sort of thing in which the biographer finds the characteristic end, desire, or purpose, which he will often take for the principal clue to the character he is studying. So far, beyond a doubt, we are still dealing with incidents of consciousness, and

---

[1] " If you want to be anything, you must become something" (HEGEL).

so far the biographer has mainly to write down what he finds in the waking mind before him.

But there is another side to this part of our subject, and it is necessary to say a word about some factors of it. I will speak, still under the present head, because it is obviously one which leads us to modify our exclusive interest in actual consciousness, of three remaining elements, three descending grades of awareness, which the biographer recognises and amply deals with in any careful study. These are—our standing world, our unconscious desires, and our body with its habits. And after speaking of them I will bring this chapter to a close by reminding the reader of the biographer's custom, pursued sometimes beyond the reader's patience, to begin the biography before his hero is born, and to extend it after. It may easily become tiresome, but the instinct which it exhibits is unquestionably sound. A man's story most certainly begins before his life, and be he great or little, known or unknown,

continues after it.   What would the story
of Christ have amounted to if it had ended
at the Cross or even at the Ascension ?

First, then, the biographer must try to
reconstitute his subject's standing world.
He cannot be conceived or understood
from isolated trains of memory, association, present perception.   He must live in
an order which is taken for granted, and
in which past, present, and future have
their recognised place.   This order, say, in
Scott's case, largely the history of Scot-
land, punctuated by the '15 and the '45,
and passing into the history of his own
day and of the Napoleonic wars, is a
standard, a persistent set of co-ordinates,
if I may be excused for using the phrase,
which enables inference, memory, perception to be arrayed without clashing, in a
past and in a present reality, which are
distinctly discriminated, but continuous
and in agreement.   This is the permanent
background of the subject's consciousness,
and it makes possible at all the points
required the insertion of particulars by

memory, communication, perception. It
is a standing criterion and a standing
receptiveness. The biographer exhibits,
throughout, his hero's more transitory
experiences as embroidered, so to speak,
on this background, and shot through and
coloured by its grain. And it is not an
accidental feature, but a conquest of the
specifically human mind, by which, unlike
an animal, it can mean and know what is
away from and removed from the present,
and may doubt what offers itself even in
given perception or claims a place in
expectation, and accept or reject it according to the standing criterion.

Here the biographer's task begins to be
very delicate. All through our account of
his work, indeed, we have seen him
struggling with the facts of latency, and
perhaps tending to underrate them; but
from this point onwards we are requiring
him to deal with something whose parts
are never explicitly present all together,
and only by nows and thens given to
clear consciousness singly. And yet in

some sense they are nearly always there. The biographer and the novelist know well, better it seems to me than the popular psychologist who talks largely of the unconscious, what it is for a suggestion to be influential " without our knowing it " or " without our attending to it." How far did Bulstrode mean murder when he handed out the key of the cellaret? How precisely is each of us affected by his knowledge that the Antipodes exist, by having heard of Einstein's theories or of the influenza epidemic, of the Washington Conference or of the famine in Russia? How were Scott's plans for Abbotsford affected by his vision of Scottish history? How do our practical plans and certainties for any coming day or week depend upon and imply the map and habitual life and routine of the countryside in which we live? Our social world seems too obvious to mention; yet it is perhaps the final and fundamental example of what we are trying to indicate. It is about our path and about our bed and spies out all our ways, and yet we are by no means always thinking about it.

Such, and of such a kind, is our permanent ideal yet independent world, the frame of reference for all our thought and perception, our memory and expectation. No biographer ignores it. I should feel on less sure ground if I were to say that no psychologist does. In considering it we are passing away from the clearest moments of explicit consciousness.

Then we are to return for a moment to the problem of desires and purposes, so far as it is relevant to our present topic of what is loosely to-day familiar as the unconscious.

Undoubtedly a purpose or desire, in its full explicit nature, involves an idea or meaning which refers to the future, and stirs to motion by its contrast with the present. But we have already noted above something by which the biographer is driven to fill out and remodel this general statement. For the " end " of which we hear is not merely at the end. Already as a forecast inherent in consciousness it is working in the consciousness, and it is not adequately described as a mere future condition, an ambition, or a guiding star. What attracts us in the future would have no interest for us unless something in the present drove us towards it ; and the biographer, who knows this well, makes it his business to show the conditions of our impelling uneasiness as well as of our guiding hope. It is easy to see that a man's world cannot stimulate him to action unless it operates in him and in his conditions as well as setting before him an idea and an aim. The path he is to follow must be where he is, as well as far beyond.

This consideration carries us further ; for if there must be a present uneasiness in desire it may be that, as we are told of instinct, the uneasiness may come first, and only after time and varied trials lead up to a recognised path which really makes for satisfaction.

This set of facts leads to all sorts of consequences, some of which are thought new to-day, and which make (I do not say unduly, in especial for practice) a great to-do in the world, and some which are as old as the hills and have long been very influential, and may be so again. We shall come across them later, and must not dwell upon them now. But it will be well to trace the bare outline of the connection.

The minimum in action is that we move to remove an uneasiness. But does this minimum include awareness even of what the uneasiness is, let alone of the real way of removing it ? Certainly not.

There are apparently all degrees, from the nesting bird, which must have, we suppose, some sense of a " not-yet," which it feels as an uneasiness or stimulus, up to the man who tells himself what he is trying to do, and says plainly what it is he desires. Throughout, awareness may largely be absent, and if present it is sure to be in some degree wrong. Why ? Because till we have got satisfaction we proceed by trial and error in looking for it, and so *ex hypothesi* are always more or less wrong.

And I suppose common experience tells us that we never get it at all complete, though about this a good deal might be said.

Now what the biographer or novelist sees, is, that a connection of this kind is double throughout. The " real " desire, inferred from the tendency of the acts, may be of a nature below, so to speak, the " conscious " desire, *i.e.* what a man tells himself is his desire. He may flatter himself in what he tells himself, and his actual movement may be selfish or cruel or sensual, while he takes it to be generous or pure. This is what the modern theorists make such a fuss about. The unconscious desire itself—very likely just the normal form of primitive desire (Russell)—is treated as a sort of secret disease—a consciousness suppressed after having been recognised. This is all very well, and may be final, and useful to be known, though it is simpler to take the " unconscious " form as natural.

But there is the opposite possibility, which is quite undoubted fact. The man may in what he tells himself not flatter himself, but may underrate or misread himself out of perplexity or blindness to, or lack of faith in, his own nature. This is the old, old doctrine that, however bad we may seem, we really pursue every aim *sub specie boni*. And it is interesting and valuable to understand that this old truth is only the counterpart of the Freudian analysis, is quite as profound, and no less practically important. Men *are* much worse than they "tell themselves," but also they are much better.

This the biographer and novelist well understands, and here, I think, he is better informed than the psycho-analyst. I quote a typical paragraph from a very great writer: "Such was the argument that Oak set outwardly before him [viz. not to let a bulk of corn be deteriorated by wet to less than half its value]. But man, even to himself, is a cryptographic page, having an ostensible writing, and another between the lines. It is possible that there was this golden legend under the utilitarian one: 'I will help to my last effort the

D

woman I have loved so dearly ' " (*Far from the Madding Crowd*).

There is the great instinct of the whole self as there are the little instincts of the partial selves. And both alike may operate without our telling ourselves that they are operating.

The problem of the detection of quasi-latent elements in desire, so far from being new, is the recognised province of the greatest dramatists and masters of fiction. And I do not much believe that, even for current apprehension, a total untraceability of the relatively unconscious causation is so common as modern theory professes. Every great dramatist and novelist teems with examples of such analysis, suggested or completed. And at what seems the uttermost extreme in opposition to consciousness, we have as an object for the biographer the hero's body. The body, to the biographer, is important in a sense in which the pure ego, if ever he heard of such a thing, is not. He does not raise any theoretical question as to whether consciousness is wholly founded on the bodily life. But he knows, as a practical man, that it is through the body, as an expression or instrument, through its appearance, its speech, its responsive habits of all kinds, that he has to bring the facts of consciousness and character before his readers. There is of course in biography, and still more in fiction, a large place left for contrast between appearance and reality, which in works of imagination is extended by the love of the marvellous. In the famous passage of the *Iliad*, from which, I take it, the fundamental antithesis, in the classification of styles of oratory, as we find it even in Quintilian, is derived, the description of Odysseus obviously implies this motive of a marvellous contrast. When Odysseus rose to speak, Antenor tells us in the *Iliad*, he would stand looking on the ground, making no movement nor gesture, so that you would take him for a fool. But when the torrent of his eloquence began, then you would feel that no man could match Odysseus.

But this is not really an exception to the law of expressiveness through the body. It is an intensification of expressiveness by art, making use of contrast. When a novelist indicates that the great soldier or the great detective is a singularly retiring and inconspicuous person, he is indirectly suggesting a special quality of force in reserve. Antenor, I should suppose, meant something of the kind. It is not that the appearance is inexpressive, it is that it is indirectly and subtly expressive.

There is something which has been insisted on as an exception. George Eliot, I think, and also Wendell Holmes, urge that you may have inherited some bodily feature, *e.g.* some facial play of muscle, which seems to proclaim sincerity, though your character may be much otherwise. Pressed far, this would bring one to an ultra-Mendelian view, that one is a composition of units independently heritable.

I do not believe the exception is important. Even if we begin more or less like that, I believe the unity of life takes

command of us throughout, and the body
has to be read in one with the mind.
We have only to think of all that the
monosyllable " health " means to the
biographer, say, again, of Walter Scott or
of Goethe, or, once more, of Keats. Any
doctor will tell you what a strain on the
heart is involved in creative work. He
has not, I repeat, as such any theory of
mind and body. But it is necessarily his
task and effort to present this as a whole,
interdependent and throwing light upon
each other. Of course there are special
cases. Could a study of Emily Brontë's
appearance help you much to the compre-
hension of her wonderful inner life ? Not
obviously, I suppose, but to a sympathetic
vision there surely would have been revealed in her something that was not
ordinary.

We have seen so far how the biographer
or imaginative creator of personalities is
bound by the necessities of his function to
work with the whole and the concrete. He
was tempted, we saw, to make too much

of consciousness, as if a receptacle in which everything lay together ; but on the whole he was right in insisting on the significance of its amplitude, and particularly on all that is implied by the phrase " enjoyment." On the unity of the person we saw that he has, on the whole, no theory ; but it is the assumption at root of the very interest on which his entire work reposes, and it is hardly going too far to say that he finds it to be founded in the solid and continuous quality, the focussed feeling, which the man before him simply *is*. And passing from the full extreme of consciousness, through the unity which underlies it, we have seen how he analyses the subtle relations of desire and instinct, conscious and unconscious, till we reach what seems to be mere fact and causality in the body which is the exterior appearance through which it all comes to be known. All these strata, we see, the biographer, real or in imagination, is forced to do justice to, to exhibit as continuous and interdependent, and to keep before his reader without intermission their most intricate and delicate reactions ; so that, although disintegrating analysis is wholly absent, yet if " a comic actor can give lessons to a parson," it appears as if, no less, a novelist could give many to a purely analytic psychologist.

4. To complete the picture, there is something more. Who has not been bored by the conscientious biographer who begins his hero's life from his great-grandfathers and great-grandmothers ? Yet his instinct is surely sound. " Anything can be cured," says Oliver Wendell Holmes, "if you send for the doctor soon enough ; but soon enough might be 200 years before the patient's birth, and we seldom send for the doctor as soon as that." And as the story-teller begins before life's beginning, so he continues after its end. The funeral, at least, the opinion of the world, the fortunes of one's children, of his writings, of his doings in the sphere of his activity—all these enter into the tale of what he was. "Our founder John Lyon and all others our benefactors, by whose benefits we are

here brought up to godliness and good learning." Does not this reference even to-day belong to the story of the founder of Harrow School ? In Herodotus' stories of the typically happy men, is it not singular, but perfectly just, that he runs on to include in their circumstances of happiness all sorts of things which never were within their personal consciousness ? The man, as a great writer has said, is the sphere " which his activity doth fill." And here again, as in that which *petitur sub specie boni*, wherein the man builds better than he knew, we have a return match of the unconscious, in which it is above and not below, the instinct and desire of which the man is able to " tell himself." Thus the impulse of the biographer bears witness to the seamless continuity by which the individual passes into the universe.

CHAPTER II

1. By the title of this chapter I mean to indicate the general view in which consciousness is distinguished throughout by its relation to an object, and in which three terms, act, content, and object, are discriminated as inherent in this relation. As I understand the matter, this conception has governed the procedure of psychology since Brentano's day, though it might not be easy to determine, with regard to some important ideas, whether they are departures from its principles, or modifications within it. The view of Prof. Stout, for example, exhibits, as he recognises, a marked affinity for it, though his dealing

with psychical content tends to destroy
the quasi-independent position assigned by
the general theory to that element in the
structure ; and the " act," also, he understands in a different sense from that upheld
by most of those who are influenced by
the point of view in question.   Those again
who claim the title of realists differ pro-
foundly among themselves with regard to
the recognition of any " act " at all—Prof.
Laird, for example, and Prof. Alexander insisting strongly on this feature of the view,
and the neo-realists on the whole rejecting it ; while another division exists with
regard to the recognition of "content,"
which, as I understand, the realist *pur
sang* refuses to distinguish from the
object as apprehended, while the critical
realist recognises it as distinct from the
" object of thought," as essence or quality.

Mr. Russell, as we shall see below, in
dealing with " the Russell Mind," rejects
the whole set of discriminations and
thus returns, though bringing with him a
radically evacuating analysis, to the naïve

standpoint of the descriptive biographer, in
so far as he refuses to break up the mind
into distinct persistent factors, other than
the psychical material—images and sensations—itself. I may as well say at once
that I am preparing no *dénoûment* in the
way of attempting a destructive criticism
aimed at Mr. Russell's view. In many
ways it seems to me clearly right and instructive as against the naïve representa-
tion of the biographer, which lays, in parts,
far too much emphasis on consciousness;
and to my mind it affords a great relief
as contrasted with the Brentano-Meinong
ideas, which seem to me to be founded on
quite unreal discriminations, and to look
for " the mind " and " the acts " altogether in the wrong place and in the wrong
phenomena. I shall indeed accuse Mr.
Russell of one fundamental vice. But this
he will appear rather to share with the
Brentano-Meinong attitude than to maintain in antagonism thereto. Neither the
one nor the other, I shall say, permits the
real world to enter by virtue of identity

into the world of knowledge. For both, the two worlds are merely parallel and similar, and their connection through " objective reference "—a phrase originally employed by myself, following in substance Mr. Bradley, with a different significance from Mr. Russell's—seems to be, alike for Mr. Russell and the other view in question, hopelessly unworkable. Still, if I had to choose, I would sooner take his view than the other. It is clean and straight, and errs, in my judgment—except in the fundamental vice which they share—much more by omission than by artificial invention. And this is a far lesser fault.

2. What is obvious in the " Brentano-Meinong mind " as contrasted with the " biographer's mind " is that the mind is no longer taken all of a piece. This was necessary, it may be said, if mind was to be scientifically studied. But it is only in a limited sense that this is true. You may analyse a concrete being into an order formed by groupings and interactions of homogeneous elements, or into a structure

containing ultimate heterogeneous factors. Of course one cannot say *a priori* which type of analysis is right ; but it is clear that they lead in very different directions.

(*a*) Mind, according to the view before us, is still taken mainly as consciousness, but it is very far from being taken as a container or receptacle. It has, to begin with, as consciousness, a peculiarity throughout which nothing else possesses ; the peculiarity of being always related, in a special way, to a something which may be called its object. It does not run on its own rails or stand on its own basis. It is " intentioned," directed towards a something which is the necessary complement of its peculiar nature and is itself a peculiar kind of being — the object of thought or desire or valuation.

Now about this relation of consciousness to an object, there seem naturally to be two possibilities which we should not prejudge. It may be inherent, as in the account of mind which we are considering ; but it also might quite well be something

very generally present, but not inherent
in consciousness, except in the sense that
it naturally grows up with the organisa-
tion of certain processes and structures
which are attended by the development of
that which more particularly is concerned
with objects, namely of *thought*.   The relation of thought to consciousness is indeed
the principal problem of the present work,
and will fall to be considered on its merits
at a later stage.

And another point arises inevitably.
This conception of an object is compatible
with very different ideas of the way in
which the psychical material, the series of
data we find in actual consciousness, is
operative in it.   A separation between the
object and the sensations or images which
represent it is an obvious and convenient
scheme.   And of this scheme the analysis
before us avails itself to the full, in the
discrimination between content and object.
The content, it seems obvious to say, is
existentially present in the mind when we
judge or feel or value.   The object, that

to which consciousness is intentionally directed, it seems equally obvious, may not be existentially present in or even before the mind. The example of a past event is the most striking and the simplest, and we will try to keep it in sight throughout any discussions on this matter. In thinking of Caesar's assassination, I certainly seem *prima facie* to have certain images in my mind to-day, but to be thinking of an event, something real and truly judged, which cannot possibly be existent in my mind to-day or take place in its presence. And the distinction between content and object enables me at least to express this apparent state of the case.

(β) This is one element discriminated by the doctrine we are speaking of, within the structure of consciousness, and in its *prima facie* obviousness there lies, I take it, a great part of the plausibility which has caused a belief in the analysis before us to prevail so widely. You cannot do without " content " in some sense or other.

There must be psychical matter in a mind. If the behaviourist denies images, yet I suppose he cannot deny what are commonly but inaccurately spoken of as sensations, that is to say, the apparently primary experiences which enter into sense-perception.

And it is probably in consequence of this obviousness of mental content as a factor in consciousness that the doctrine affirms its second discriminated element, the act. What I mean by saying that the assumption of this element probably followed from the apparent obviousness of the content, is simple. The content includes *ex hypothesi* all distinguishable particulars that are present when consciousness is directed to an object. If, then, we are desirous still to attach some meaning to the transitive form which seems natural in describing the mind's relation " to an object "—it affirms, desires, esteems, or what not—we have left ourselves nothing in particular to serve as its character or vehicle. So all we can say is that besides the content and the object there is an

" act " by which consciousness envisages
an object which may be absent—we are
to bear in mind the past event. And this
act, whatever the content or the object
with which it deals, is always in itself the
same. Naturally so, for everything that
could distinguish it falls in the content.
Attempts to give the act a character not
simply borrowed from the content with
which it deals are familiar in such theories
as those of Prof. Laird and Prof. Alexander,
and are said to be supported by introspection. But there is no unanimity as to
their existence ; and to me, I must confess, an act of thought of any kind, which
has a nature pure and simple of itself,
apart from that of the " sensations,"
images, or object, which it is supposed to
be attending to, is wholly unintelligible
and incredible. I cannot find any trace
of it in introspection, nor have I been able
to attach a meaning to the accounts of
it which I read in Prof. Alexander and
Prof. Laird.

(γ) As regards the object, the third term

E

of the discriminative analysis we are considering, we have noted the plausibility of the view before us. We have a certain " content " existentially in our mind, and by help of it we enter into some sort of relation with an object, say once more, an event in the past, which is not and cannot be a factor or constituent of our knowledge. The relation may be described, for example, as one of similarity. I have existentially in my mind an image of a man being murdered in an ancient-looking building among a number of men who wore gowns, and I believe that something like this happened a long time ago and was and is called the murder of Caesar. But then we pay for the simplicity of the scheme by the difficulty of holding its parts together so as to satisfy our real belief. In a common sense-perception we are not aware of anything like this separation between content and object. The object is clothed in its content, and what we say of it, we say of the single thing before us, not of a something remote which

is like a something else at home which we
have existentially in our minds. Now let
the object be removed from us, or we from
it, in space or time. Is there any difference
of principle ? Surely, none at all. What
we describe as a thing or narrate as an
event, is still in just the same relation to
us as what we saw with our eyes. We
think of the train we saw start from King's
Cross in just the same way when we believe
it to be at Grantham, and in the same way
again when we affirm that it has reached
Edinburgh. The reality seems to work in
our consciousness ; it exercises control,
and, remaining itself, yet modifies itself in
virtue of connection with the other objects
which make up our world of reality.
There is no point at which we make a step
from an image to an object resembling it.
Somehow—it may be difficult to explain—
but somehow, plainly, the real objects and
events remain as immediately what we
think of, what we talk about and affirm
or deny things of, as anything which we
touch or see. I speak of Caesar's murder,

and I mean Caesar's murder. I do not
mean something like a mental image, which
somehow corresponds to it. I mean an
event in the real world, which is itself
a constituent of my affirmation about
it. What I have in consciousness helps
me to think about it; but what I
think about is not what I possess at
the moment in consciousness; not a
" content."

We may illustrate by raising the question of proof. If we do not get to the
past event by a jump from similar content
to similar occurrence, how do we get to
it ? By memory ? Not in most cases nor
ultimately. The typical and ultimate
process is proof, to which memory is akin,
so far as it is based on and extends the
present reality. Now the noticeable point
is this, that in proof of fact we never at
any point depart from the real world.
However remote in time or space may be
the fact, it is always, if established, established as an amplification belonging to the
same world which we presuppose and

specify in setting out to prove it. If we are aware of a house, we say it had a builder; and we think as directly of the builder as of the house itself, even if the house is in Crete and the builder is of about the age of Minos. We may know next to nothing about him; but he, and not something existentially present in our minds, is as definitely the object of our thought as the house on the faith of which we believe in him or as the house in which we live to-day. The case which Mr. Russell specially notes is in truth universally typical. " To revert to the noise of the tram, when you hear it and say ' tram,' the noise and the word are both sensations (if you actually pronounce the word), but the noise is part of the fact which makes your belief true, whereas the word is not part of this fact. . . . Thus the word occurs in the belief as a symbol, in virtue of its meaning, whereas the noise enters into both the belief and its objective."[1] The fact which makes your belief

[1] *Analysis of Mind*, p. 239.

true (I should say your "judgment," for I
hold it an error to identify judgment and
belief) always and without exception in
some measure enters into your judgment
—is a constituent in the judgment. That
it is not an actual sense-perception (mis-
called " sensation ") can make no difference ; for, as we saw, in establishing our
judgment we never break contact with our
real world. The builder is as real as the
house, and the builder's grandfather as the
builder, and all of them as the noise we
hear the tram making. On p. 270 Mr.
Russell gives an excellent description of
proof by correlation of facts (by coherence),
which shows exactly how in establishing a
fact you go back and about to exhibit it
as of one piece with your present world—
as undetachable from it. His denial of
coherence as the test of truth, in face of
such a passage as this, is clearly shown to
rest on misunderstanding.

Thus it is plain that the separation of
content and object of thought, whether
in the Brentano-Meinong account of the

mind, or in the recent Critical Realism,[1] in spite of its plausibility and convenience, is altogether untenable. Prof. Stout's well-known view[2] will serve for a criticism upon it and an amendment of it.

3. If the distinction of " act," " content," and " object," on which the Brentano-Meinong view of mind reposes, is, as we have thought, untenable in the unverifiability of its " act " of mind, no less than in the separate being of content and object, is there nothing which is to be called an act of mind? This would be contrary to our feeling. We shall see that even Mr. Russell, who is hard to persuade that mental elements exist, counts belief to be a verifiable mental act. And we shall do well to set before us a passage from Prof. Stout,[3] which helps us to a definite line of departure from the Brentano-Meinong mind:

"I had not originally (*i.e.* in *Analytic*

---

[1] See my *Meeting of Extremes in Contemporary Philosophy*.

[2] See, *e.g.*, *Some Fundamental Points in the Theory of Knowledge*, MacLehose, 1911.

[3] *Op. cit.* p. 4.

Psychology) any single word to designate
what have since been called ' acts.' I
was content to describe them as ways of
being conscious of objects, or as attitudes
of consciousness towards its object. I
would now reserve for them exclusively
the title of *subjective* states or processes ;
for presentations are not predicates of the
subject in its individual unity and identity,
as believing and being pleased are. The
term ' act ' is certainly convenient, and
in view of its having already become
current, I am prepared to accept it. But
in doing so I make two reservations. In
the first place, I would make a distinction
between acts such as supposing, believing,
or desiring, and the relation to an object
which is common to all. All acts as such
involve this relation, but it is not itself an
act. It is not itself a mental state or process, but a relational attribute of certain
mental states or processes. In the second
place, the word ' act ' must not be taken to
signify activity ; it is sometimes maintained that activity is not to be found in

our mental life at all, and though I heartily disagree with this position, the question is one which I do not propose to discuss on this occasion. But in any case I submit that if the mind is, properly speaking, active, it is so only in virtue of one kind of ' act,' that in which it is interested in an object as something to be sought or shunned. Mental activity, therefore, if there be such a thing, must be identified with conation, the striving aspect of our conscious life." The presentative function of presentations, it should be explained, which here Prof. Stout discriminates from what should be called an act, is for him to " specify the direction of thought to objects, so that the nature of the presented object varies in correspondence with the varying nature of the presentation."

This, for him, is not to be an " act " of mind. There is no act in which the mind is, properly speaking, " active " except conation.

Here at least we know where we are and get away from the colourless " act " of the Brentano-Meinong mind, which is distinct over against content and object. We want the act, if, as seems to be required by language and feeling, there is to be an act at all,—we want it to be a feat of the mind " in its unity and identity," and to be exhibited in some change or movement in which it behaves somehow towards its objects, its real world. I use the word *behaves* as a very general term, just because it seems to me that we may have to go back on Prof. Stout's refusal to regard the relation to an object as an act of mind. Conation itself will seem, perhaps, to belong to a wider category than the word directly designates.

Surely the typical and fundamental act of mind is that self-assertion of the object by which, through the mind and by means of its psychical matter, it asserts and constructs itself, and controls the mental behaviour, both theoretical and practical. The key word, which must here be introduced, is the word *thought*, the relation of which to consciousness demands investigation.   We are at once brought up against a paradox.   If thought is the control of the mind by the object, and this control is *the* act *par excellence* of the mind, then *the* act *par excellence* of the mind is not its own.   That is to say, thought rather governs consciousness than is an act of consciousness.

For instance, you have a pain.   That is *prima facie* hardly a thought, except as inevitably from the first you in some degree fix the ways and degrees in which it asserts itself.   It is more naturally " a mere feeling."   But now suppose it is persistent, localises itself, has a character by which it is recognisable and which reproduces in your mind symptoms which you have known before, and which indicate further symptoms to be expected.   These disagreeable anticipations prove true ; and on the other hand efforts at amelioration, such as have proved helpful in your own experience or in the doctor's, are not effective, but the expectations based on them fall to the ground and are abandoned.

Here the feeling has maintained itself as a discriminated and self-consistent object. It takes charge of your course of presentations; unites itself with some of them, which it reinforces and modifies, and which modify and reinforce it; enfeebles and expels others, at the expense of which it develops its own characteristics and becomes prevalent and dominant in consciousness as the knowledge of an attack or illness of some definite kind.

What is all this self-assertion, union or fusion, extension and enlargement in harmony with a persistent character, rejection of some offered presentations and ideal suggestions, and acceptance of others, which remodels the whole mind and mental contents under a control emanating from a single complex through a principle of coherence and consistent self-development? Its name is the monosyllable to which we referred above; it is what we call "thought," and all these self-maintenances and fusions and modifications—responses graduated and qualified in accordance with quantitative and qualitative stimuli—all these are what outside psychology, and when their nature is fully exhibited, we call judgment and inference.

I was going to have said, what I think would in the main have been true, that here we have got a distinct step beyond the biographer and the poet.   I think that as a rule they would represent thought as essentially one with mind considered as consciousness, and would not realise the paradox which we are intending to confront.   But their field of observation is so wide, and so unfettered by theory, that you cannot, so to speak, safely trust them to be wrong.   In Rosalind's father when the peasant lad reminds him of his daughter, in Gloster when unawares in company with Edgar, in Jock Jabos when he recognises young Bertram as " auld Ellangowan arisen from the dead," we note the recognition of " mnemic causation," with that effect of a surprise sprung on consciousness which we know so well in ourselves, and which is so characteristic of thought even in its highest stages. Its beginnings go right down into the world of instinctive response to identical or proportional stimulus, so that not I only, but better authorities,[1] have been willing to take habit as at least a felicitous equivalent for the universal in which thought is operative.

" A surprise sprung on consciousness " —is it not so ? The felicitous comparison, the " happy thought," the appropriate hypothesis—you cannot make them come, by any exhibition of what your consciousness contains. " Postea in mentem venit," says Cicero, in narrating a purely legal argument which developed itself in his mind.[2] The case in question, enlarging itself by mnemic causation through legal reasons akin to it, determined the path of his consciousness, not *vice versa*. It is not necessary to insist, surely, on the apparent miracles of what is commonly called association, where the line of connection is untraceable, though the appropriateness of the

[1] *E.g.* Alexander and references in *Implication.*
[2] *Letters to Atticus.*

connection when brought into consciousness is undeniable. Striking examples are
to be found when verbal similarity is wholly
excluded, as between passages in different
languages, as when modern religious ideas
recall the faith of the experienced Ulysses
compared with the timid distrust of the
young Telemachus.[1]

Then is thought merely what used to be
called association ? Is not that to reduce it
to the level of fancy, however capricious ?
I suppose the answer is that thought is
association, understood as the marriage of
universals or development of connections,
in as far as this displays self-maintenance.
It displays self-maintenance, as we saw,
because the object, which operates in it, is
persistent and consistent, and nourishes
itself, so to speak, out of the psychical
material which it meets with, taking what
agrees with its growth, and rejecting what
it cannot assimilate.

---

[1] *Odyssey.* The point is that here a whole seems to link
itself with another whole through character, by felicitous
suggestion. There are no " similar " particulars.

Much would have to be said, if we were treating at all fully of thought for its own sake, about its relation to supposition and imagination. But here it is enough to point out that though undoubtedly thought may make assumed or ideal positions its starting-point, it cannot but develop them according to the laws of logic—which are the expression of central characters of reality— and the nature of things so far as not specially determined in the assumed starting-point. If fresh assumption is intruded on the process after the starting-point, the thread is broken, and the conclusion is not drawn but fancied or supposed.[1]

But here we are speaking primarily of the relation of thought to consciousness. And we say that the germ of thought is present in the formation of habit as a practical recognition of universal connections in reality and a response and modification in accordance with them. Certainly it seems present in the higher animal world, and it is, in essence, rather the precursor

[1] See *Implication*, chap. viii.

and perhaps the generator of consciousness than anything which is an operation springing from the material present in consciousness itself.

The universal relation of consciousness to an object then, which the Brentano-Meinong theory insists upon, is, I should urge, less correctly attributed to consciousness than to the presence of thought throughout consciousness. On the other hand, as thought, I should have said that it ought to be treated as an act, if there is to be any act of mind at all, and not, as in the passage quoted from Prof. Stout, to be regarded as a mere relation which is shared by consciousness in all its forms.

For thought, as the development and self - maintenance of the object in ideal form, is, essentially, the judgment. And the judgment is surely the central act by which reality, operating in and through the mind, becomes a constituent of knowledge and of action.

In a certain sense no doubt it is true that conation is the central character of

F

mind, and that it is only as conation that mind can be said to exert activity. But I question whether, if we understand by this activity something separately discriminated as conation and set over against thought, we have got the true kinship in view.

The distinction between thought and conation is surely superficial. All thought is the self-maintenance of universals, and every universal is on one side a conation. Every universal is a growing creature. It tends to extend, to ramify, to specify, differentiate, and adapt itself. By tending to do so, I mean (following Mr. Bradley) that it does so if not inhibited. The process by which an idea gains predominance in the self and passes into act is not essentially different from that by which it gains predominance in the intelligence and passes into theory. The processes not only are precisely parallel, but they constantly exhibit the characteristic features of each other, and the distinction between them is, it may be said with a useful exaggeration, accidental. By accidental I mean that it depends on the obstruction which the developing object chances to meet with. When we note that huge practical activities —costly and laborious expeditions—are undertaken for such ends as the verification of Einstein's theories, it seems needless to insist on the minor cases which attend us all in our most ordinary theoretical activity—looking at the clock if we want to know the time, going to fetch a book if we are held up by ignorance of a fact or argument. Obviously and beyond dispute the growing and coherent object of thought can dictate any step within our mental and physical resources, and it is a mere matter of degree when we call one amplification of it—mainly ideal—theoretical; and another—mainly translated into external movement—practical.

The one genuine distinction which might be said fairly to hold between them is, I think, this. We call any activity theoretical if its guiding clue is an interest in the further determination of an experience

as yet very imperfectly determined, however much external effort directed to
specific change of conditions may be needed
for the task ; we call any activity practical
which has for its end the achievement of
a condition already conceived as determinate, however much determination of
indeterminate factors may be indispensable
to the procedure as a whole. Obviously
the' two characteristics may be combined in
any degree, the one as means and the other
as end. And we know that means and end
are not absolutely distinguishable, and that
each colours the other. We may set out
to test Einstein's theory by a result, as
yet undecided, which only a specific highly
determinate enterprise can elicit ; we may
throw ourself into the adventure of pacify-
ing a distracted nation, knowing only that
we mean to do it somehow, without seeing
in the least beforehand how we shall have
to set about it. The former problem is
ultimately theoretical though the means in
the main are practical ; the latter is ultimately practical, though it involves as a

means a difficult theoretical investigation into the conditions to be satisfied. The difference is between getting a decision and doing what is decided.

Though the indeterminateness makes the theoretical character, yet it is plain that in every theoretical stage there must be a limitation *ad hoc* of the immediate object of research; and this must always constitute a degree of affinity between the practical and the theoretical condition. If we act from a known want, it is conation; and thus, if we know what we want to know, as we always in some degree must, and act from that want, then we bring our theoretical effort explicitly under the head of conation. In a word, we may say that in theory, as in practice, we are always solving a problem; and the attempt to solve a problem may always be considered as conation.

Thus we seem to be led to a view of the mind which escapes from the artificial and empty analysis of the Brentano-Meinong doctrine, but in a certain sense admits a concept of act or activity which though equally concerned, as that of Prof. Stout, with the concrete mind in its fulness, yet has, owing to its generality, a kinship with what he sets down as a mere relation of mind to object, distinct from the conative attitude which alone seems to him to be an act of mind in a proper sense. It rather looks, to us, as though the essential and fundamental activity of mind were co-incident with thought, and thought again were coincident with the relation to an object which penetrates, not necessarily all psychical life, but all forms of it sufficiently developed to be considered as consciousness. And this pressure or energy of thought, the essence of which is the nisus to the whole or to individualisation,[1] is again identical with conation in the widest and proper sense, in which it includes the double aspect of theory and practice.

Thought, then, we say, is the fundamental act or activity in knowledge,

---

[1] Cf. for this and for the view here expressed Bradley in *Mind*, 1887, p. 354 ff., " Association and Thought."

practice, and valuation. *Whose* act or activity is it ? We sympathise with the naïve description of the mind as consciousness rather than with the analysis of it into act, content, and object, which seemed to us to be determined in the main by a plausible but ultimately unworkable scheme for treating the mind's relation to absent objects. But yet we are not prepared to say that thought is the act or activity of consciousness as such. At least, by consciousness in the sense of our first chapter, we mean a loosely connected bundle of psychical occurrences, mainly sensations and images, pleasures and pains, emotions and appetites, with the distinction of subject and object either absent, or being occasionally attained and lost again, or fairly established. If we take " a mind " as = consciousness thus understood, and it is thus that in everyday life we mostly do take " a mind," we cannot well say that thought is the act of mind, or that mind exercises any act at all.

The relation of thought to mind is, as

we suggested above, paradoxical. Following the track of our analysis of thought, we should be led on to say that thought is the self-assertion of reality according to its characteristic laws within a complex of psychical matter which may be called a mind. We saw that the characteristic procedure, the integration, the ramification and modification, the inhibition of conflicting elements, is apparently there from the beginning, and where the beginning is we cannot say. It is hardly thought when a bird nests in the spring under the influence of climatic change, without any trace of suggestion from previous experience.[1] But suppose it were true that a bird should pick up a feather to build into its nest ; and then reject it and fetch moss instead because of some dim preference or repugnance emanating from the qualities of the two materials. Would not this be a modification of choice effected by the control of the object over the course of

[1] If you take in heredity, and read successive lives as one, you would have to admit learning by experience at a much lower point.

psychical (say here perceptual) suggestion ? It would presumably persist, and the nest would take rank as a structure to be built with moss and not with feathers, and this would become a rule of the object, and would expand into consequences and corollaries. I do not say this account could be true ; but if it, or anything like it, were true, surely it would be a case of thought. And it would rather be building up the consciousness than enacted by the consciousness. It would retain the one nisus, and reject the other, and so start on the shaping of a mind.

Then are we to say boldly that thought as judgment and inference, in the nisus to individualisation, is the act of reality in its ideal form ? If we were to say it, we should only be repeating what I at least said many years ago,[1] and what I fully believe to be true. When I say that I think or judge, or, in what we have seen to be a parallel and kindred process, that I act in pursuit of an end, that I will or

[1] *Logic* [2], i. Cf. Russell, *Analysis of Mind*, p. 18.

desire, we are using expressions which if fully understood are equivalent to the expression the reality completes itself in and through me either in purely ideal form —what we call knowledge—or attended by various degrees of external movement, which we call action. I say "attended by," for the essential point of action, I presume all but extreme behaviourists are agreed, is will. And if there is no specification of ideas through thought towards the end of action, there is neither action nor will.

Two questions seem here to press upon us. Why do we so strongly and naturally feel and affirm that it is *we* who think in thought and act in action ; or in our more accurate statement, that it is *we* who are conative in all conation ? And further, the question we have had in prospect all through, What is the relation of thought to consciousness ? It is the answer to the second question that must be the complete answer to the first ; but the first can be approached *prima facie* by a simple statement. What thinks, we may say, to express roughly the fundamental and guiding truth, is myself rather than my mind ; and it is myself that thinks because it is the living and growing real which I have built up and am building up *par excellence* as my world. Whether I say Law is not antagonistic to freedom, or I throw all my active powers into opposing a protectionist candidate at an election, the process is essentially the same in character. It is the organised and persistent object, built up as the centre of my standing self, which takes charge and by its selection of what is consistent with itself and its rejection of what, considering the whole situation, is inconsistent with it, guides consciousness into the thought or action which constitutes the judgment or the practical response. *I* think so or act so because what I am shapes itself so. If any one asks whether this allows of freedom, I can here only give him the old answer : he who talks of freedom and excludes thought knows not what he says.

Then for our second question, which seems to me to go to the bottom of the whole problem, and which lays the foundation for dealing in the following chapter with " the Russell mind."   What has mind or consciousness to do with thought ? Admitting dispositions, organised tendencies of some sort which are not maintained in consciousness, why should not thought according to our account be a habit of selection and modification producing responses from the total organism appropriate to the environment at any moment ? Why do we lay the enormous emphasis on consciousness that we do ?   I suppose the answer is that consciousness enables thought to operate on a far more extensive and a remoter field than mere habit can, by presenting a vast number of alternatives, absent no less than present, to selective attention.   Attention, I take it, is one key-word to the value of consciousness, and enjoyment is the other.   I mean, primarily, enjoyment in the natural sense, though I should have no objection to approaching Alexander's use of the term as a description. But enjoyment in the natural sense is the great and paramount blessing which we owe to consciousness, as attention is the secret of its causal efficacy. By consciousness, the universe, and not merely what we touch or even see, is opened to our attention, and the ramifying and self-moulding body of our ideal and actual world nourishes and develops itself on what is appropriate to it in this enormous field, through the operation of thought as it exercises selective attention as a basis for creative construction. These last words indicate to us a subject which we shall enter upon after treating of the Russell mind.

CHAPTER III

THE RUSSELL MIND

Consciousness not Essence of Mind.—1. The mind as represented by the novelist or biographer, and the mind as represented by the followers of Brentano, have at least one main characteristic in common. In both of them we are primarily face to face with consciousness. We saw, indeed, in considering some developments of the Brentano position, that a point of view was arising from which consciousness might appear as a way or connection in which, under certain conditions, objects were related or interdependent, rather than as a peculiar gift or magic exercised by a unitary being, or some sort of stuff or medium lying over against the world of

78

things, somewhat as a mirror or mirage lies over against the world it reflects.

In Mr. Russell's account of the mind we are refreshed and stimulated by beginning, at all events, from quite the other end.

Greatly influenced by behaviourism, he insists on it first and last, that consciousness is not the main differentiation of mind. " Consciousness is a complex and far from universal characteristic of mental phenomena," and " Mind is a matter of degree, chiefly exemplified in number and complexity of habits." What we actually observe in mind are trains of particulars— particulars of external action, of sensations, and of images. Everything else in mind which we are accustomed to consider that we are aware of, is built up out of particulars such as these. We need not speak just now of the idea that such particulars, taken apart from special conditions which bring them into mind, may be the ultimate reality of the universe—a " neutral stuff," in which both the physical and the psychical world have their roots. What interests us at present is the simple contention that we can discover in mind nothing but trains of particulars, and that thought and knowledge, for example, and consciousness where consciousness is admitted to exist, are nothing but habits and complications into which such particulars are built up.

And I will explain at once in general the attitude which I shall adopt towards this contention. I shall urge that it is right in about one-half of its thesis, but that this its element of truth does not justify its negatives. In minimising the presence of knowledge and thought at least, it appears to me that the theory is influenced by antiquated notions of their nature, so that it looks for them where no sane doctrine would expect them to be found, and fails to observe them in the very phenomena by which it labours to replace them. I will begin by setting out in a quotation from Lotze's *Logic* the essential point of the considerations which I mean to urge in criticising the doctrine.

It will follow, if I am right, that Mr. Russell's analysis will help us to dismiss a great deal of equivocal talk and antiquated lumber ; while at the same time something further will be indispensable to complete his account of mind into a reasonable conception.

Consider the passage (Lotze's *Logic*, sect. 339) : " The point I wish to emphasise is that a general conception, even if we consider merely its content at any one moment, indicates a task which no actual idea, that can be presented to the mind, can fulfil " [eine in wirklicher Vorstellung unerfüllbare Aufgabe].

What I understand this to mean is that the universal or the operation of thought or reason is not to be looked for in anything presented as a single fact, *in propria persona*, so to speak, for consciousness. Always it remains true, as Hume affirmed and Mr. Russell maintains, that what we light upon in the process of consciousness is a something particular.[1] The operation

___

[1] *Logic* [2], i. 38, x.

of thought is not to be looked for in
generalities or abstractions presented as
such to the mind, but in the " use " made
of particulars as indicating a meaning,
in the "control" exercised by the object
upon their trains and their reinforcements
of each other, in the " habits " which
reveal themselves in the responses of the
organism to particular stimuli which possess
a certain identity.   To illustrate, as do the
behaviourists and Mr. Russell, the universal
of thought by the phenomena of habit is
in no way a new departure.   The present
writer asserted in his *Logic* (1888) that
" An idea or concept is not an image,
though it may make use of images.   It is
a habit of judging with reference to a certain identity." [1]   And Mr. Bradley goes, as
it seems to me, to the heart of the matter
when he writes (*Essays on Truth and
Reality*, p. 309) : " The universal, and even
our awareness of it, come in my view long
before language is developed.   As soon as
one has with anything the sense of same-

[1] *Logic* [2], i. 38.

ness or familiarity, with and over against the sense of difference or novelty, one is, I should say, aware of a universal. On the other hand, I agree that it is only through language that the universal becomes known as such "; or p. 298: " Suppose that on an object of a certain kind you are accustomed to act, practically or theoretically, in a special manner. So far you may know nothing about any universal, though obviously there is here a universal, which you use, or which uses you, in a certain fashion. Then let us suppose that there comes a striking difference in the instance. Upon this you hesitate perhaps, and then proceed to act in your usual way. Still this noticed difference may have its effect, and may lead to a consciousness of ' and yet ' or ' after all.' You are now aware of a sameness, and, with it, a difference which is there and does not count. But this sameness is a basis which, as such, is not before you. It is felt, as that which is in one with the habitual use which later is named." All this of course is intimately connected with Mr. Bradley's well-known criticism of the association theory in the *Principles of Logic*. The importance of all this in relation to the doctrines of Mr. Russell's book is that we see clearly in what sense we are free to affirm (1) that the operation of something akin to thought and of the nature of habit is long anterior to explicit consciousness (that animals, for example, do what is equivalent to reasoning and inference, though it is probable that they are aware of no clear distinction between ideas and reality), and (2) that even in the world of the developed human consciousness we are not to look for thought as a mental presentation *sui generis*, as *e.g.* in pure abstract ideas, but we are still to discover it in its laws and operations, working as it were behind the scenes, and governing the emphases and successions and structural relations of the particulars which we are at every moment discerning and discriminating within the inseparable unity given in our psychical material. Thus we

are prepared to say with Mr. Russell that
the analysis of mind discloses nothing but
particulars ; only we must add, except
the unity which is fundamental to them,
and reveals itself throughout in the laws
of their interconnection, though its operation is at least as much akin to habit as
to consciousness, and the former charac-
terises mind at a much earlier stage, and
perhaps more intimately, than the latter.

The reference to habit in elucidation of
the nature and operation of the universal
is accepted by Professor Alexander in his
important work *Space, Time, and Deity*,[1]
and, in fact, is a perfectly obvious consideration.

No doubt it raises interesting problems
as to the point in the ascent towards explicit intelligence at which mind is to be
held to begin. But to recognise this in
agreement with Mr. Russell[2] as a matter
of degree on which definition must be to
some extent arbitrary, or determined by

---

[1] Alexander, *Space, Time, and Deity*, i. 214, 235.
[2] Pp. 307-8.

our special purpose, is an attitude necessary to the rational treatment of mind in
the face of all the facts familiar to us
to-day. It is plain, as the present writer
has urged at length,[1] that whatever our
ultimate view may be as to the position of
mind in the universe, it does not come
before us, in the animal world, except as
something which arises, so to speak, on
the top of a vast evolution, and presupposes a long development of connections
and formation of dispositions, by help of
which alone the principle which far down
operates as if it were thought, can create
for itself a field of consciousness, and a self
which is formed and full of determinations
before it is aware of them or of its own
distinct existence. This, I think, is the
sort of way in which Mr. Russell would
wish us to approach the relation of mind
to habit and to consciousness. And in
this, I believe, he is right. All the same,
the operation of thought is plainly manifest
in mind, if you know where to look for it.

[1] *Principle.*

The difficulty, indeed, as the present writer has indicated,[1] is a real one ; and Mr. Russell has done very good service in pointing it out. " All that is observed and discovered is a certain set of habits in the use of words. The thoughts (if any) in the mind of the examinee are of no interest to the examiner ; nor has the examiner any reason to suppose even the most successful examinee capable of even the smallest amount of thought." [2] There can be no doubt, I think, that there is talking and writing of which this is true, or all but true. A man may really repeat a conjunction of words from a mere wish to be talking or writing, with no guide but a dim reproduction of conjunctions of words which he has met with before. Or, at a slightly higher level, he may argue from a general proposition simply because he has heard argument based upon it before, without the smallest appreciation of any correlations in reality which sup-

[1] *E.g.* on second-hand inference and low-grade thinking in *Knowledge and Reality*.
[2] P. 29.

port the argument and give it a distinct reference. Nevertheless even an examiner is not so forsaken of heaven as to be wholly unable to see where thought is present. The creative spirit of language, by which its growth and ramifications are made, when thought controls them, to pursue a course always a little new and vitally springing from the old, appeals to the sympathetic mind just as the living plant is discriminated from a dry stick. Mr. Russell himself, in his treatment of knowledge, to a great extent shows how.[1] But the contention is sound that mind is a matter of degree. Only it is a mistake to use the obviousness of this position to cast doubt on the higher degrees.

2. Now let us look at some examples of the attempt to display the mind as built up out of mere particulars, mere sensations, and images. Let us take four central cases of mental functioning: (a) Belief; (β) Memory; (γ) Meaning and Truth; (δ) Thought; and try to see how a complete

---

[1] Cf. Lecture XIII. on accuracy and appropriateness.

account of them, while justifying the importance assigned by Mr. Russell to " particulars," nevertheless discovers in these functions something very much more.

(*a*) Mr. Russell's treatment of belief at once displays the essence of his doctrine in its general nature.   But it will be necessary to follow up in some little detail the other functions above mentioned, in order to see his exact position at the chief critical point.

We may clear out of the way at starting the objection which any one must feel, who cares for precision of language, to treating belief as practically equal to assertion or to propositions.   It is noticeable that, as we often find with Mr. Russell, he corrects this erroneous usage, which as a rule he adopts, in a passing paragraph.[1]   We must distinguish, he points out, between " belief as a mere disposition and actual active belief.   We speak as if we always believed that Charles I. was executed, but that only means that we are always ready to believe it when the subject comes up."   This

[1] P. 245.

seems to admit, in passing, the true
doctrine, that belief is psychological, and
has degrees, while judgment is logical
and is taken as infallible while it stands.
For our purpose, however, we need not
insist further on this distinction. What
Mr. Russell is discussing is " actual active
belief," which he means to be equivalent
to what we call judgment or assertion.

" Just as words are characterised by
meaning, so beliefs are characterised by
truth or falsehood. And just as meaning
consists in relation to the object meant, so
truth and falsehood consist in relation to
something that lies outside the belief." [1]

This gives at once the essential point,
which we have only to develop. We see
that we are called on to accept a distinction
closely analogous to that which seemed so
plausible in the Brentano-Meinong doctrine. This resemblance Mr. Russell fully
recognises. The contrast of content and
object is fundamental to him. His whole
conception of knowledge, in which belief is

[1] P. 231.

a central point, depends upon it. Acts, indeed, he rejects in general ; but he makes an exception in favour of belief, which is an actual experienced feeling, involving the three elements of believing, what is believed, and the objective. And the distinction between content and object, that is, in his language[1] between what is believed and the objective, is indispensable to him.

And the reason is obvious, and is this : " What is believed, and the believing, must both consist of present occurrences in the believer, no matter what may be the objective of the belief. Suppose I believe, for example, that ' Caesar crossed the Rubicon.' The objective of my belief is an event which happened long ago, which I never saw and do not remember. This event itself is not in my mind when I believe that it happened. It is not correct to say that I am believing the actual event; what I am believing is something now in my mind, something related to the event

---

[1] P. 233.

(in a way which we shall investigate in
Lecture XIII.), but obviously not to be
confounded with the event, since the event
is not occurring now but the believing is." [1]
The fact, then, or event, that makes a
belief true or false, and to which the belief
has the relation called objective reference,
is something "that lies outside the belief." [2]
"You may believe that such-and-such a
horse will win the Derby. The time comes,
and your horse wins or does not win ;
according to the outcome, your belief was
true or false." I have dealt with this view
at length elsewhere ; [3] but it seems ad-
visable to suggest here also, before going
further, that even in common usage it will
not carry you all the way. In strong cases
of a " true " belief for a wrong reason, the
wrongness of the reason is felt to inter-
fere with the truth of the belief. If you
chose your winner from having dreamed
his name, perhaps it would be held right
to say your belief was true, though
obviously its truth was a fluke. But sup-

<hr>

[1] Pp. 233-34.   [2] Pp. 231-32.   [3] *Logic* [2], ii.

pose, on a foggy day, I go down to the 11 A.M. train, and find a train, and it takes me where I want to go; but it is not " the 11 o'clock," but " the 9 o'clock " two hours late; surely then my belief that I should catch " the 11 o'clock " was false. It rested on the normal arrangement, and as a belief in this it was false. It did well enough by a fluke. The falsehood of the reason begins to gnaw away the completeness of the correspondence with fact. There is a sort of correspondence, but it is not with the fact as you meant it. It does not go far. Or suppose a man told me " There is a train at nine "; so I went down and found a train, but was told the nine train was off, and this was an excursion special which happened to run in at that time. Surely I should tell my informant " You were quite wrong; the nine o'clock is taken off; luckily I got a special that was passing." Usage does not support the theory after the first look. Truth must carry you some way.

But for Mr. Russell's theory of belief,

and of all the functions which it determines, this separateness of belief and object is essential. Knowledge involves no more unity with its object than there is between a signpost and the town to which it points.[1]

In harmony with this view, when we look closer at the nature of a belief, we find that it is indeed always complex, being in fact of the nature of a judgment, but always has a content consisting of words only, or of images only, or of a mixture of the two, or of either or both together with one or more sensations.[2] But it cannot consist of sensations alone except in so far as the sensations are signs. The content must be kept separate from the objective. They are parallel but cannot meet.

It seems to me very remarkable that one of the cases which Mr. Russell mentions, which shows the objective entering into the content in its own right, though it is true of course that the content, as in any judgment, must include a symbol of

[1] P. 235.   [2] P. 236.

an idea (*i.e.* the content cannot be composed wholly of sensations in their own right), is simply " ignored for the sake of simplicity." It is the case mentioned above, in which " sensations in their own right form part of the content of a belief." [1] When you hear the noise of a tram, and say " tram," the noise is part of the fact which makes your belief true, whereas the word tram is not part of this fact. " The noise enters into both the belief and its objective." If we generalised this experience, as we remarked above, we should get a theory of belief opposed to Mr. Russell's. We should say that the reality is always a constituent of the judgment.

Our purpose, however, is to draw out the peculiarity of Mr. Russell's own theory. And for him the fundamental point is that belief consists of a complex of particulars, together with a certain feeling, called a belief-feeling, which is a complex of sensations demanding analysis. The content and the belief - feeling must not merely

[1] P. 239.

co-exist. There must be a specific relation between them, to the effect that the content is what is believed. This, like the belief-feeling itself, seems to be postulated, but left unanalysed.

Thus we have on our hands as the factor of belief a series of mental particulars with objective reference, and a belief-feeling in a special relation to them. Obviously all turns on the nature or conditions of the objective reference. But before proceeding to trace this further in the main functions of belief, memory, meaning, truth, and thought, we must pause to notice one pregnant view to which Mr. Russell is much inclined, and which, like that about sensations which form part of both objective and belief, ought to carry him away from the position in which we find him.

It is the view that a sole alternative must be affirmed, which Mr. Russell takes from Spinoza's statement, approved by James.[1] It is a well-known view, but it is curious to see how it is distorted when

[1] P. 248.

combined with Mr. Russell's doctrine. Mr. Russell, we have seen, finds in belief a specific feeling, plus complexes of particulars, images, words or sensations. For him, then, the result of Spinoza's view would be that the specific feeling can be dispensed with, and that "the mere existence of images yields all that is required." [1] The interest of this attitude for us is the strong light that it throws on his idea that belief, if the specific feeling were taken away, must fall back simply into the existence of mental particulars. The conception that belief, the acceptance as fact of all suggestions which the felt present does not exclude, and the impossibility of entertaining suggestions which the present rejects, is indigenous to the mind from the beginning, does not occur to him. And therefore, while rightly interpreting Spinoza's thesis to imply that "Doubt, suspense of judgment and disbelief all seem later and more complex than a wholly unreflecting assent," he holds that by accepting it he would be

[1] Pp. 248-49.

H

driven back to the opinion that " an un-
combated image has the force of a belief."
And this assumption, he argues, would only
explain very simple phenomena. It would
not, for instance, explain memory nor pure
theoretical beliefs, such as those of mathe-
matics. All this is due to his working
with mental images instead of thoughts
of objects. Starting from the latter, one
finds it the plain rule that belief is prior
to disbelief, as thought is operative from
the dawn of mind, and that there is no
meaning in setting up the mere existence
of images as a phase in mental development
at all, nor any reason for refusing to recognise naïve thought (his " existence of
images ") in the beginnings of memory as
of all the assertory functions, *e.g.* expectation and bare assent which he classes with
memory under the head of belief. Spinoza's
view, when rightly stated, expresses a
fundamental truth, and the author's difficulty in adopting it arises wholly from his
restricting mind to mental particulars plus
feeling.

(β) We may pass to the consideration of memory from a text of the lecture on Belief.[1] " When a person has a memory-image with a memory-belief, the belief is ' this occurred' in the sense explained in Lecture IX. [which deals with Memory] ; and ' this occurred ' is not simple."

Here we are at the point we want to develop. When we express our belief of a past event in such words as " this occurred," what exactly do we mean ? For if we know this, we know the meaning of " objective reference," or the relation between the mental particulars which are the content of the belief and the objective which makes it true or false.

Here is the passage from the lecture on Memory.[2] " The memory - belief confers upon the memory-image something which we may call ' meaning ' ; it makes us feel that the image points to an object which existed in the past. In order to deal with this topic we must consider the verbal expression of the memory-belief. We might

---

[1] P. 236. See p. 89 *supra*.   [2] P. 179.

be tempted to put the memory - belief into the words ' Something like this image occurred.' But such words would be very far from an accurate translation of the simplest kind of memory-belief. In the simplest kind of memory we are not aware of the difference between an image and the sensation which it copies, which may be called its ' prototype.' When the image is before us, we judge rather ' this occurred.' The image is not distinguished from the object which existed in the past; the word ' this ' covers both and enables us to have a memory - belief which does not introduce the complicated notion ' something like this.'

" It might be objected that, if we judge ' this occurred,' when in fact ' this ' is a present image, we judge falsely, and the memory - image, so interpreted, becomes deceptive.[1] This, however, would be a mistake, produced by attempting to give to words a precision which they do not possess when used by unsophisticated

[1] Cf. p. 171.

people. It is true that the image is not absolutely identical with its prototype, and if the word ' this ' meant the image to the exclusion of everything else, the judgment 'this occurred' would be false. But identity is a precise conception, and no word, in ordinary speech, stands for anything precise. Ordinary speech does not distinguish between identity and close similarity. A word always applies, not only to one particular, but to a group of associated particulars, which are not re-cognised as multiple in common thought or speech. Thus primitive memory, when it judges that ' this occurred,' is vague, not false." Of the " this " as here used "contradictory predicates are true simul-taneously ; this existed and does not exist, since it is a thing remembered, but also this exists and did not exist, since it is a present image." Hence arise Hegelian "identity-in-diversity and a host of other notions which are thought to be profound because they are obscure and confused." " When we become precise, our remembering becomes different from that of ordinary life, and if we forget this we shall go wrong in the analysis of ordinary memory."

It was worth while to make this long quotation, for it gives us the whole paradox in a nut-shell. We wanted to know how the content of belief, present in particulars within the mind, enables us to make assertions about the object which is past and in reality. And the answer is plain. Our normal memory rests on a confusion which we do not notice. We confuse two similars, the present memory-image and the past object. If we did not confuse them our judgment " this occurred " would be false. If our remembering were raised to the level of precision, our phrase would be " Something like this occurred," where " this " is the memory-image.

Two things are plain at once. (i.) The operative bond between content and object is similarity. (ii.) This does not justify a direct affirmation that the object occurred, unless the relation is unnoticed, and object and content are confused. Of course this

must be so if we will have no constituent
in memory but mental particulars, and the
real object must fall outside the assertion,
as a town is outside the sign-post which
points to it.

And the confusion works even more
strongly. The memory-image, which is all
we actually have, " would not be said to
occur " (in the crude use of the word,
which is what concerns us).[1]   It would not
be noticed at all. For occurrence means
having a context of correlations, of the
sort that constitute physical objects. The
prototype has these, the image has not.[2]
So the " this " not merely confuses image
and object, but predicates of the confused
totality what could not possibly be true of
the image, to which alone, if we were
accurate, it could refer, but only of the
objects. The feeling of reality is a feeling
implying or suggesting the presence of such
correlations, by which reality can have
effects on us without our co-operation.
This feeling is what we have when we say

[1] P. 184.   [2] P. 185.

a thing occurs or is real, and, once more, this is something we could not possibly say of the image. It is plain that on Mr. Russell's view we only have normal and true memory, which is of objects, by help of a confusion. When we learn to speak accurately (of " *something like* this ") our " this " has lost its objective reference, and is no longer joined to the object we once perceived.

We must pursue further, under the head of memory, the consequences of reducing the mind to a train or trains of particulars. It will be evident to every instructed reader that in commenting on Mr. Russell's account of memory I have in mind, for comparison, Mr. Bradley's elaborate analysis in chaps. xii. and xiii. of *Essays on Truth and Reality*. And the general thesis which I want to insist on is not so much that Mr. Russell's account is wrong in comparison with Mr. Bradley's, as that there is so very little of it. He seems to start from his ultra-simple hypothesis of the mind-memory, *e.g.* as first sensations

and then images accompanied by belief,
and expectation as first images accompanied by belief, and then (in the verification) sensations.[1] He does not back up
his theory by any explanation of the sort
of evolution which such a phenomenon
as memory presupposes in the history of
mind, or any reference to the aspect of
the developed world of knowledge in which
it is interwoven and apart from which it
could not exist.

Thus, to begin with, when he mentions
the quite obviously imaginable hypothesis
that the world sprang into being five
minutes ago, exactly as it then was, with
a population that " remembered " a wholly
unreal past, he does not point out the grade
of inconceivability of this idea which arises
from the essential nature of memory itself,
as our experience reveals it to us from
day to day. The hypothesis would be
just on a level with that old superstition that the world was created with
all the geological record ready made,

[1] P. 269.

fossils and all, to try, or to support, our faith.

Memory involves habits, dispositions, acquired discriminations and points of view, as much as a fossil involves the past life of an organism. You can suppose either created at one blow, but in doing so you are contradicting what current experience teaches us of their nature. Mr. Russell speaks as if, with a mind made up of sensations and images, it was merely a matter of fancy to suppose that memory-belief originated at one blow, and an orderly past, present, and future established.

But the thing is self-contradictory, not merely very improbable. In order to have true memory, that is, a definite recollection of objects and events in our past experience, and more or less accurately dated, you must have certain definite acquirements. It is not enough to have habit and associated particulars. Here Mr. Russell, I think, agrees. You must identify and place the past event, and not merely do

something which it has helped you to learn
to do. In a word, you must judge. You
must have gained the conception of an
order reaching beyond your present and
personal world, and liable to conflict with
it ; and you must be capable of referring
the objects of your thought to places in this
real and independent order. This implies,
if the nature of mind is to be explained
consistently with everyday experience, a
long preparation and growth in the machinery by which, as we see daily, the mind's
mature work is carried on. We need not
discuss at this point Mr. Russell's assertion
that there is no logically necessary connection between events at different times,
though it obviously rests on a dualism
which would exclude the notion of necessity from scientific inference in general.
But as regards the nature of mind itself,
the comparison made above is perfectly
just. The structure of mind which admits
of true memory as strongly demands a
precedent evolution of mechanism, as the
fossil record demands a previous life of

organisms. You can imagine an immediate creation of either, but under penalty
of destroying its intelligibility. And if
we are to undertake the analysis of mind
at all, we must avoid assuming such a
contradiction *ab initio*.

We may illustrate this nakedness of
Mr. Russell's treatment by his comparisons
of the animal mind to that of man.
Whether in the responses that in some
sense indicate a universal,[1] or in the question as to the possession of true memory
in however simple a form,[2] there is the
same facile ignoring of the acquisitions
which mind in its maturity displays. The
second point will suffice for an illustration.
" There is no reason why memory-images,
accompanied by that very simple belief-
feeling which we decided to be the essence
of memory, should not have occurred
before language arose ; indeed, it would
be rash to assert positively that memory
of this sort does not occur among the
higher animals." Now I have said that

[1] Pp. 228-29.   [2] P. 242.

I think Mr. Russell is right in holding that mind is a matter of degree, and consists largely in habits, and therefore extends far down into the organic world, and below what we commonly call explicit consciousness. But this admission ought not to make us careless about its phases.

The simplest form of true belief-feeling, which is the essence of memory, I understand to have place for Mr. Russell when we "feel that the image points to an object which existed in the past." [1] The recognition of an order of things which includes a past contrasted with the present is thus an acquisition which is a condition precedent of true memory. And it is an acquisition which the animal mind shows no signs of having made. It is " a hard and late achievement of the mind," conditioned in the main by language. " It is this ideal order which makes memory possible, and apart from this development to postulate memory is to invoke a senseless miracle." [2] Of course a conception like this involves a

[1] P. 179.   [2] Bradley, *Essays*, pp. 336-37.

theory of ideas and of judgment and of the nature of the world as experienced by the animal and the super-animal mind respectively. All I am doing is to point out that you cannot reasonably take the mind, reduced to trains of particulars, and extract from this bare skeleton of it a theory of its mature functions, without considering the achievements and acquired points of view which make the functions possible. Mr. Russell himself distinguishes well and clearly between true memory of events in the past, and the results of mnemic causation such as Semon in the main discusses ; and we are merely demanding that the same respect for the maturity of mind should be preserved in the rest of the analysis.

Let us follow the same thought further. Confining himself to the assumption of mind as constituted by bare sensations and images, and complexes of them operating as feelings, Mr. Russell, in order to account for true memory, has a question to face which develops into two others.

(i.) " Why do we believe that images are, sometimes or always, approximately or exactly, copies of sensations ? What sort of evidence is there, and what sort of evidence is logically possible ? "[1] " How then are we to find any way of comparing the present image and the past sensation ? "[2]

On Mr. Russell's assumptions as to the nature of mind, as constituted wholly by particulars, and as to the relation between content and object, the content being present in the mind, and the object being past and outside it, there is no possible answer to this question except on the lines which Mr. Russell adopts, dealing exclusively with characteristics discoverable in the images themselves. To this explanation we will return directly, merely pointing out at present that the necessity for it arises immediately from the nakedness of the mental land as revealed by Mr. Russell's survey. The difficulty is the same, of course, as that which is the main

---

[1] P. 149.   [2] P. 161.

argument for subjective idealism, that you cannot compare your sense-perception with the real object which you assert it to indicate, and therefore you cannot possibly know either that the one is like or that it is unlike the other. And the solution is the same, and as simple. It is in recognising the work of thought, not as affirming abstractions and entities beyond experience, but as dealing with unities revealed in the nexus of actual experience, *qua* real objects in the real world.

A man, we will say, saw, a fortnight ago, and never before or since, a house in which he is much interested, as he is likely to live there for the rest of his life. He now has a memory-image of it. What right has he to say that the memory-image resembles the actual house, or, indeed, is an image *of* it at all? The answer is that when he saw it, it was not a mere image, but an object of thought which he construed to himself with the help of a visual perception, and of course, in real experience, of many more sense-perceptions and motor sensations, focussed in a centre of reference, which was the object of thought, *i.e.* the house.

When he got into the cab and came away, the object, the house, did not cease to be an object to his thought; it did not drop into the status of an image or a number of images (that it always would involve at least a considerable number of images of different kinds taken in connection is an important practical detail). It remains the house, an object in the real world, construed or referred to by help of the surviving images of all kinds, but, essentially, known as the real thing in the real world which they refer to and indicate, just as much as the house in which the man is living when he thinks of the other is an object to his thought. His thought moves in the world of real objects, and has never come out of it. He thinks of the house he saw, and reconstructs it to his thought out of all the psychical material he brought away and connects with it, relying on certain cardinal relations with his ideal world in general for its identification with what he saw and its distinction from other houses, *e.g.* on its number in a street or its distances from familiar points.

Now if we ask " How like is his recollection of the house he once saw and is so much interested in, to the house as it really is ? " the answer is in principle that we cannot possibly tell. If he has seen half-a-dozen houses on the same day, any amount of confusion may have introduced itself into his memory. Say he has bought one of the houses. He may have mentally endowed the house he has bought with the kitchen he has seen in some other house, and the garden he has seen at yet another. All you can say is, that he is thinking about some houses that he has seen, and if the one he has bought does not possess the feature his memory-image ascribes to it, he will be a good deal astonished when he again looks at his bargain. But the point is that what he is doing is thinking of a house and trying to recall the features by which he described it to himself. And as a rule he will recall images enough of salient features to distinguish the house from others and make it serve as a focus for his memory as that object which is indicated to him by certain features. What he knows is that his images are *of* the house ; for they are so, by the fact of his referring them to it, even if they are wrong. If he has put in the wrong kitchen, we say his idea *of* the house is mistaken. But this is what we know ; that his idea is *of* the house. If we think his images altogether wrong, we may indeed say " Why, you are thinking of another house." But what does the wrong or other house mean ? It means " not the house we were both *ab initio* referring to." Thus the phrase shows that the reference to the object is still presupposed. *How* like the house his image may be we cannot possibly say, except by taking his description and comparing it with the house itself ; which in the case of a past event or object become inaccessible is of course impossible. But even when two objects have been confused there is a continuity with the original object of thought, however transformed *en route*. The idea is *of* what it has been attached to throughout in thought.

Mr. Russell, as we said, answers his question differently.   For him, necessarily, the memory - images must in themselves have two characteristics by which we can arrange them in two series, of which one corresponds to the more or less remote period in the past to which they refer, and the other to our greater or less confidence in their accuracy.

(ii.) Our confidence or the reverse in their accuracy, then, Mr. Russell contends, is based on the feeling of familiarity that accompanies them.   " In an image of a well-known face, for example, some parts may feel more familiar than others ; when this happens, we have more belief in the accuracy of the familiar parts than in that of the unfamiliar parts." [1]   Mr. Russell opposes this explanation to " some image-less memory with which we compare them,"

[1] P. 161.

as if this were the sole alternative, as indeed on his assumptions it is. But familiarity is of course a most fallible symptom of trustworthiness. What it indicates is that something, though presented without preparation, comes home to us as if it had been expected. It betrays the existence of a disposition favourable to it. But how the disposition came to pass, whether from a previous experience of the prototype of the image, or from some working of the imagination, or some interest in a characteristic that may be generally distributed (*e.g.* in the style common to the portraits of a particular period), it is impossible to judge on the ground of familiarity alone. There are many signs which influence us in accepting the fidelity of a memory-image, and this is one of them. But it is nothing in the least approaching what can be called a criterion.

(iii.) The characteristic of images which makes us regard them " as referring to some more or less remote portions of the past," taken as a feeling attaching to the image itself, "may be a specific feeling which could be called the feeling of past-ness." [1]   But it must strike the reader how at this point but little stress is laid on this feeling, and how the author goes on at once to the characteristic of context, which though in one case he takes it as a memory of process in an order mediated by the mark of just-pastness in " akoluthic sensa-tions as they fade," yet forms a transition to a wholly different way of explaining our faith in memory and our sense of pastness in its objects.

To understand this we have only to return to the point developed in criticising the assumption stated in (i.), out of which (ii.) and (iii.) inevitably sprang.

Memory, we said, works in the real world.   Its objects are objects which have been, and continue to be, the objects of our thought, to which it is essential to conceive a world in its unity.   It operates therefore on the basis of our acquired judgment and conception of a systematic

[1] P. 162.

order of things, extending, through past, present, and future, to a place in which the objects of true memory (as apart from the previous experiences which only give rise to habit) are *ipso facto* referred with more or less explicitness. The first thing of all is (and this fundamental point Mr. Russell refers to in passing, after his custom [1]) that the past, though real, excludes and is excluded by the present. The event remembered is one which could not be now. How does the man know that the day he saw his house is a fortnight back ? Because he was in London on that day, and has not been so in the fortnight since. Further, the context of true memory is partly, as Mr. Russell well says, a successive context. You start from a present base of suggestion, you may jump to your remembered event which at first you only know to be excluded by the present, but before you have finished placing it you have recalled the series of steps which links it with the present, and

[1] P. 178.

which, being facts of the standing world of your knowledge and recognition, give it relations and a date.

And the same account gives the rationale of accuracy. It, no less than pastness, depends on context. Memory is indeed not pure inference, because at some point a simple perception, not in a necessary sequence of condition and consequent, enters into it. From the fact that the man was standing in the road before his new house, he can draw no inference that it had outside shutters. It was, as we say, a chance, whether, having every opportunity, he noticed them or not. But, as we argued before, the apprehension from which his memory derives was certainly defined and reinforced in all sorts of ways by the systematic world in which he located it. You may say that these things are not memory but knowledge. But supposing that they all were present and co-operated in the apprehension, how draw the line between ? We go everywhere and think of everything, in various degrees, within a scheme laid out and pre-perceptive. Take the most private of private recollections. A man remembers to have been furiously angry at a remark of a fellow-schoolboy some sixty years ago. He never told any one. No one but himself experienced it. But the occasion drops at once into its place in his life - world. The background and content were part of the event, and of themselves date, place, and define the occurrence. *E.g.* the feature " fellow-schoolboy " fixes limits of date on it at once. Certainly memory is fallible, and he may have imported into the situation, in later reflection, elements supplied by subsequent inference. Nevertheless, the conditions of such an occurrence are typical conditions of memory. You go to it on the basis of the present, and from the present ; which both furnishes your starting-point, and excludes from itself, to a determinate extent, your remembered fact. We may refer, by anticipation, to Mr. Russell's account of verification,[1] to which

[1] P. 270.

we shall have to return.   He applies it to
matters beyond our recollection, to truth
in general.   But it applies within the limits
of memory to our confidence in its accuracy,
and his appeal to context in treating of
memory starts on a path which ends in
verification in treating of truth.   Additions
by subsequent inference are not memory.
But context or correlations which formed
part of the original apprehension as deter-
mining the object certainly are so, though
they may be more as well.   A man's early
home, for instance, which he may have left
fifty years ago, is to him absolutely the
centre of a map and the counterpart of a
constructive plan, and the nucleus of a
great complex of personal relations.   Such
an object may be extended at the edges into
later knowledge and inference ; but surely,
if the main part of it is not memory, there
is no memory worth having at all.

These considerations we pursued as an
elucidation of the bareness and unsup-
portedness of the mental functions when
conceived as merely the operation of trains

of sensations and images which come to us with certain sorts of feelings.

I shall now recur somewhat more briefly, in completing the criticism of the author's account of memory, to what has already been referred to in his explanation of the memory-belief, in its character as a present occurrence related to a past event. This character, outlined as we have seen in the chapters on Belief and Memory, I shall afterwards study more in detail in the fuller analyses which are offered as throwing light on " Meaning and Truth," and on " Thought."

First, then, we must notice that the general type of the counter - view which I have used in criticising Mr. Russell's approach to his theory appears to him to be incompatible with the repudiation of a " subject " or an " act " in knowledge. " We could then have said that remembering is a direct relation between the present act or subject and the past occurrence remembered : the act of remembering is present, though its object is past. But the rejection of the subject renders some more complicated theory necessary. Remembering has to be a present occurrence resembling, or related to, what is remembered." [1]

Now we remark, to begin with, that for Mr. Russell belief is an exception to the rule that acts must be rejected. For belief is an actual experienced feeling, and contains very similar elements to those which constitute the Brentano-Meinong " acts." [2] Why then cannot belief, as an act, be directly related to the past or absent object ? Apparently because (compare the criticism of Prof. Stout's views [3]) such a relation involves some survival of the notion of a " subject " or " single observer." But here, as so constantly, Mr. Russell inserts the thin end of the hostile wedge into his own argument, for " introspection " is all that Prof. Stout requires, and Mr. Russell points out that you may very well believe in introspection without believing in a single observer. [4]

[1] P. 163.   [2] P. 233.   [3] Pp. 110-14.   [4] P. 114.

Obviously you may, and Mr. Russell's difficulty arises from an obsolete notion of the nature of thought, which he appears to suppose to be conceived as the mystic act of a unitary being, a sort of angel inside the mind, or as a peculiar staff or medium with qualities like a kind of magic mirror. But if we take thought, as I understand philosophy to take it, as the manner of operation by which, in a mature mind with a long evolution behind it, the laws of mnemic causation determine the maintenance and recognition of objects in experience, then I cannot see why the resultant of such operations should not be an assertion in which the mind, being a co-operative unit, shapes, or is shaped by, its experience as affirming a determinate real world. The laws in question work towards unity and completeness ; that is a matter of observation and experience ; and the mind as a whole in which psychical material is controlled towards unity by the laws in question is what we mean by the mind as thinking. By thinking it orders its objects in a world, and I cannot see why this world should not remain present to it, so far as psychical material—feeling and sense-perception—offers the occasion. The objection to the act of thought, the self-maintenance of the mind as a whole, from antiquated ideas that it presupposes a single agent or subject, seems to me altogether without application to thought as philosophy conceives it.

Thus, then, to put in a few words the essential result of the discussion of memory on Mr. Russell's basis, " primitive memory when it judges that ' this occurred ' is vague, but not false." [1]   Primitive memory is what we are dealing with in the discussion ; [2] in refined or reflective memory we have a further step in which the relation of object to image, as we saw above, is no longer presupposed through absence of distinction, but is replaced by a relation of similarity.[3]   We can then say, *i.e.* speak-

[1] *Op. cit.* p. 180, cf. *supra.*
[2] Cf. p. 185, " In the crude use of the word (occurs), which is what concerns us, memory-images would not be noticed in themselves."   [3] P. 179.

ing reflectively,[1] " that the image " means " the past event." [1] But really, as our previous discussion showed, in this reflective memory, on Mr. Russell's view, the relation just previously mentioned as meaning or expressed by the word " of " in the phrase " image *of* " is simply destroyed, and is replaced by a relation of similarity, which is quite different. We analysed [2] the reference to an object of thought by help of an image, and we saw that it was the true relation in memory and judgment which on Mr. Russell's basis can only be accounted for as a confusion. The question of course is that concerning identity.[3] For us, Mr. Russell's primitive judgment gives the nature of objective reference rightly and truly. As it is modified according to him by reflective discrimination that nature abandons it wholly, and it becomes false. The true sense of " of " vanishes, and what remains, the relation of similarity, being wholly undefined, and its affirmation

[1] P. 187. [2] Pp. 112 ff., *supra.*
[3] P. 180. Cf. *supra.*

consequential upon the recognition of the
" of," now abandoned, ceases altogether
to explain objective reference, or to bind
object and content together. It was the
" of " that did so, and the " of " is gone.

The reference to the past, we should
observe, is thrown into the belief-feeling as
opposed to the content.[1] This is again a
sign of the barrenness of the land according
to the doctrine before us. Of course, as
we saw, the conditions which make memory
possible carry with them the fact and
degree of reference to the past. True
memory means assigning something its
place in the past. Our feeling may be
affected by the process ; but the conditions
are systematic and objective.

(γ) We must now pursue the same problem—the relation of content to object, in
the lectures which deal with Meaning and
Truth. It is not to our purpose to scruti-
nise the entire detail of either lecture,
which contains much that is suggestive and
valuable ; though most of this tends to

[1] P. 186.

drive the author beyond his position. We may note, *e.g.*, the point that individuality is not constituted by similarities but by causal relations.[1] This makes a wide breach in the doctrine that systems of particulars (what we, with human thought and vision, and not those of a fly, take as given realities) are bound together by a similarity sufficient to pass as identity,[2] and replaces this by a bond of a different nature, whether or no it is really reducible to causality.

In the discussion of meaning (*Words* and Meaning is the primary subject of the lecture) we note the same characteristic which was obvious in the discussion of memory. The simple account from which the author begins is in both cases true. Memory tells us " This occurred." Meaning is what you have when " something now sensible—a spoken word, a picture, a gesture, or what not "—calls " up the idea of something else." We only get into trouble when we ask what sort of object

[1] Pp. 192-93.   [2] P. 171.

K

is called up, and how it is related to the
" sensible " which evokes it. The mainly
behaviourist account of meaning [1] which
follows on the above description seems true
and simple enough. You possess meaning
—understand a word—when it produces
in you an appropriate response. This term
appropriateness we shall meet with again
in the account of truth. It indicates *prima
facie* the place of purpose in understanding,
and introduces us to the conception that
the word can share the effects of the object
so far as these are mnemic effects. At this
point, in the fourth category of behaviourist
understanding, we begin to slide into the
fallacious track, as is indicated by the observation just referred to. The word can
acquire effects " identical with, or similar
to, the effects which the object itself might
have." [2] And this is not, as the beginning
of the lecture would suggest to us,[3] because
the word means or suggests the object
owing to previous experience, and the
suggestion of the object produces these

[1] Pp. 197-200.   [2] P. 200.   [3] See above.

effects. It is, as here we only begin to see, but shall see quite explicitly in a moment, rather because the word has by association with the object (as explained at first) acquired these similar effects, that it is at this point and later to be held to mean the object. The word is not to have the similar effects because it is the sign of the object, though apparently it is thus that it must have acquired them. It is to be the sign of the object because it has these similar effects. Obviously the theory must develop thus if it is to adhere to its fundamental principle, that is to say, that the content, which is the sign, and the object, which is the reality referred to, are to remain apart, on parallel tracks which never meet, the one in the mind and in the present, the other outside it and may be in the past or future.

Passing on from the above, the demonstrative use of language, which is more easily explained on behaviourist lines, to the imaginative and narrative uses of language, we find a marked development in the direction specified. The discussion is conducted in terms of the relation of words and images, not of words and objects. Its aim is to establish against the behaviourists the normal necessity of mental images in narration and imagination. And this thesis is sound ; but it is not sound to imply that what we describe or imagine is an image *per se*, and not an object thought by help of an image. The image in imagination, we are told, has no " prototype." Surely this is a fundamental error. The image is mental machinery, and imagination uses it in the description of objects just as memory does ; the objects are *prima facie* real, like any others ; that we imagine them and do not hold them " actual " is a special attitude of mind which needs special conditions and presuppositions. Hamlet is an object of thought with his place in the universe, referred to by help of our infinitely varying mental images just as is Alexander the Great. Who thinks of Gurth as a mental image ?

But soon we are driven to make another step. Words can mean images, we are told, and images can mean words.[1] But images can have meaning apart from words.[2] In this case, what is their meaning ? If it is " a memory-image " of " a particular occurrence, accompanied by a meaning-belief, (it) may be said to mean the occurrence *of*[3] which it is an image." But this " of " evidently rests on likeness, not on associative reference. For an image, it is admitted, often does not possess the former. And if so, its meaning is *prima facie* destroyed ; " the meaning of an image, if defined by relation to the proto- type, is vague ; there is not one definite prototype, but a number, none of which is copied exactly." The reduction of meaning in this case to a parallelism of similars has brought us to a *cul de sac*, and another plan must be tried. It is now pointed out that though the image may not be in an assignable degree like the prototype, yet its causal efficacy may be like that of the

[1] P. 206.   [2] P. 207.   [3] My italics.

prototype, and because of *this* resemblance it may mean the prototype ; and the generality or particularity of these effects may even determine what prototype it means, whether *e.g.* a particular dog or dogs in general.[1]

Thus we conclude, " In order to define the meaning of an image we have to take account both of its resemblance to one or more prototypes and of its causal efficacy."[2] This is, in other words, to take account of the resemblance of itself to the prototype, or of its effects to those of the prototype. The link is resemblance throughout.

This same principle, we now find, we are to extend to the account of meaning in general.[3] When, in mnemic causation, an image or word has the same or very nearly the same effect as would belong to some object, say, a certain dog, we say that the image or word means that object.[4] For words, this explanation is especially necessary, because the meaning of a word as a rule cannot be constituted in any

---

[1] P. 208.   [2] *Ibid.*   [3] P. 209.   [4] *Ibid.*

degree by likeness, but is wholly constituted by mnemic causal laws, owing to
which, *e.g.*, the word " dog," not being in
the least like a dog, has yet effects which
resemble the effects of a dog in certain
respects. It may be directly associated
with images of what it means, but this
is not necessary. If a word is correctly
associated with other words, we possess its
theoretical meaning; if with other bodily
movements, its practical meaning.[1]

Thus, as in the treatment of memory,
we see how the Brentano-Meinong doctrine
of mind perpetuates itself in the theory
which Mr. Russell advocates. In both
cases [2] the originally given " of," which
means that the name or image " of " an
object of thought is something by help of
which we know it the object, and continue
to refer to it and think about it, is refined
away in deference to the necessity of keep-
ing the content mental and present, and
the object real and possibly absent. The
characteristic of thought, as reference to

[1] Pp. 210-11.   [2] See p. 54 above.

some element of a systematic world, is extruded, and in place of it we have mental content and real object each running on its own rails, and connected either as in images, both by likeness of sign to signified, and by likeness of the sign's mnemic effects to those of the signified; or in case of words, where the former is as a rule impossible, by the resemblance of the mnemic effects of the sign to the mnemic effects of the signified.

But here, we urge, the real relation is inverted. The image or word does not mean the object because it or its effects resemble the object or its effects. The image is presumed to resemble the object (the presumption being unverifiable where its truth would be most valuable) because it is the image *of* the object; and the image or word actually has effects resembling those of the object (or as the phrase sometimes runs, " has *the effects, which* the object would have " [1]) because the image is the image " of " the object, and the

[1] P. 208.

word is the name " of " it. The resemblance is due to the meaning or presumed from it, not *vice versa.* The account both of memory and of meaning begins right and ends wrong ; [1] because the action of thought is first tacitly presupposed and then ignored.

It is not necessary to follow up all the details of Lecture XIII., " On Truth and Falsehood." It is perfectly plain from pp. 273-74, read in connection with p. 278, that the ideal of a true proposition is furnished by the simple case in which " we can say that true propositions actually resemble their objectives in a way in which false propositions do not." [2] What the theory would like to get in all cases is a proposition in which image is related to image, as term to term in the objective, or word conjoined to word by a word meaning a relation, as term is connected with term

[1] P. 126 above.

[2] P. 273, and note the warning on p. 212, most curious in connection with pp. 273 ff., against " assuming too close a parallelism between facts and the sentences which assert them."

by the relation itself. And this doctrine is maintained in spite of two complications : first, that propositions cannot thus correspond with negative facts,[1] and second, that the relation of the terms of the objective cannot always be represented even in an image-proposition by the same relation of the images. " The act of comparison implied in our judgment, [say in comparing sunshine and moonshine, when either image may happen to be the brighter] is something more than the mere coexistence of two images, one of which is in fact brighter than the other." [2]

Both of these complications are removed at once if we note that a judgment is not a relation between two psychical images or ideas,[3] but is the assertion of a single meaning, however complex its structure, about reality. It was long ago pointed out that in saying the earth goes round

---

[1] P. 276.   [2] P. 277.
[3] Cf. Bradley's *Principles of Logic* [2], vol. i. p. 12 : " We shall always go wrong unless we remember that the relations within the content of any meaning, however complex, are still not relations between mental existences."

the sun we do not say that the image of the earth goes round the image of the sun.[1] And so with the negative fact. In a negative judgment we predicate an alternative, particular or general—an " other " as Plato taught—defined by relation to a specified term, of the reality about which we are speaking. There is in neither case any question of resemblance between proposition and fact. The proposition is true " of " the reality because it contains a meaning united with it by thought, as in the plain sense-perception which we saw perpetuating itself in memory.[2] For the doctrine we have been discussing such a nexus is inconceivable. For such a nexus requires the object of thought to be a constituent of the judgment.

The formal correspondence in which truth for Mr. Russell's theory consists, accounts for the difficulty which it finds in dealing with objective reference. The objective reference of a true proposition is in its correspondence to fact. It involves

[1] Author's *Logic* [2], i. 76.   [2] See above.

a true affirmation. But what is the objective reference of a false proposition? There is no false fact to which it can correspond; and therefore a false proposition, it would seem, can have no meaning. Mr. Russell deals with this situation by a metaphor. The objective of the true and false proposition with the same terms is the same; but the true proposition points towards it and the false points from it.[1]

This is because, in the absolute correspondence of mental to factual particulars, which constitute, according to the theory, both meaning and truth, there is no room for meaning apart from truth. But the original use of the expression objective reference in my work on *Logic* [2] was expressly framed to meet this difficulty, and I venture to think that Mr. Russell's departure from my usage is not an improvement. How can a false proposition have a meaning, seeing that it cannot represent a fact? How can a meaning be a meaning, except by standing for a fact?

[1] Pp. 272-73.   [2] *Logic* [2], i. 4-5.

The term objective reference was framed, following the line of the footnote on p. 4 of Mr. Bradley's *Principles of Logic*, to meet this paradox. Objective reference, involved in the meaning of isolated significant signs, was to be reference to facts taken as isolated or conditioned ; assertion, the proposition, was reference to facts in their place in the one system of reality. Conditioned or isolated facts furnish the false objectives, whose existence Mr. Russell denies, to which false propositions correspond. Facts in their true systematic relations supply the objectives with which true propositions are in correspondence. Mere meaning, mere objective reference, is admittedly conditional. Truth, reference to reality, is in intention absolute. When the conditional is asserted as absolute you have falsehoods. When I say on Wednesday, " To-day is Tuesday," I take Tuesday, which is *per se* a conditional or isolated fact, the meaning of an idea we entertain or suppose or even (as in this case) could truly deny, and I attach it absolutely to a point of the real world which repudiates it, so that each jars and conflicts with practically all the characteristics of the other. Tuesday, which is a perfectly good fact when considered in its right place, as after Monday and before Wednesday, etc., becomes a false fact when asserted without its conditions and in defiance of them, *e.g.* as absolutely identified with a to-day which is Wednesday.

Ultimately, I hold, meaning does imply assertion ; and no sign could have significance unless it referred to something which is implied to be somehow and under some conditions truly affirmed as a being in reality. But in " objective reference " it is taken, by a convention or abstraction, as not affirmed but only entertained, and is not considered as referred to reality, but only to an element of reality considered in isolation. Mr. Russell's theory of truth, which consists in an equation, so to speak, of single signs of fact to single facts, and of single signs of relation to single relations, destroys this

vital distinction between isolated or conditional facts and facts affirmed or uncon-
ditionally stated, and therefore that between objective reference and affirmation.
All facts for him being thus equally true
facts, he cannot discover the source of the
false objective which gives meaning to the
terms of the false proposition. The simple
solution lies in the truth that error is the
predication as absolute (= unconditional)
of what is only conditional.

This consideration of the systematic
nature of reality as evinced in the distinction between truth and falsehood brings
me to Mr. Russell's treatment of coherence.
I have elsewhere remarked [1] on his extraordinary attitude to coherence, and have
hitherto been wholly unable to understand
it. He holds [2] that according to the theory
(of coherence) the necessity of empirical
observation ought to be denied, though he
admits that it is not. He identifies the
conception with the attempt to deduce
the world by pure thought, and continues

---

[1] *E.g., Journal of Philosophy.*   [2] *P. 268.*

to comment in this strain, which, as I say, I have never been able in the least to understand. He would seem, if it were not incredible, to repose on the antiquated antithesis of pure thought and experience, of *a priori* and *a posteriori*, and to suppose that thought means something other than seeing progressively the necessity of a whole as experience enables you to determine and complete its system.

And I now see, from the total absence of *rapprochement* on his side between coherence and verification, the close affinity of which, to say the least, must strike every reader of his book, that the point for him lies in his narrow and rigid conception of logic. Coherence, he says, exaggerates the powers of logic.[1] There is no logically necessary connection, he holds, between events at different times.[2] The existence and persistence of causal laws is a fortunate accident,[3] and how long it will continue we cannot tell. What all this means must be, I presume, that he really believes in

[1] P. 267.　　　[2] P. 159.　　　[3] P. 271.

the distinction between *a priori* and *a posteriori*, and thinks that if we had a criterion of truth in logical coherence, it ought to be infallible[1] and to operate in total independence of experience.

Therefore the account of verification,[2] which seems to the reader to be so obviously a case of coherence, is, I can only suppose, for Mr. Russell, extra-logical; whereas coherence, he must hold, claims to be logical *a priori* and infallible. This explains the curious emphasis laid on the feeling of expectation and its fulfilment, the restriction of consequen*ts* which can aid in verification[3] to consequen*ces* future to the matter to be verified, and the depreciatory reference, quoted above, to the causal laws which are used in the verificatory process.

Ultimately the only case of verification, we are told in this passage, consists in the

---

[1] P. 269.   [2] Pp. 269-71.

[3] The logical relation of antecedent and consequen*t* is of course not one of cause and temporal consequen*ce*. I doubt if Mill is clear that the logical relation of antecedence is not temporal.

happening of something expected. " We have first an expectation, then an occurrence with the feeling of expectedness related to memory of the expectation. This whole experience, when it occurs, may be defined as verification, and as constituting the truth of the expectation." So when you look up a familiar quotation, find it in the expected words, and in the expected part of the book.

Surely this is a superfluous introduction of feeling and reference to the future into a simple logical relation. Something has suggested an idea to you, and something else—this is the fundamental point for logic—confirms it. The something else must be in the future *ad hominem,* so to speak, because there must be something to confirm before anything else can confirm it. But the future has no further prerogative than this implies ; and the feeling of expectation is wholly irrelevant.

If you find a "stranger" in a cup of tea or a candle, and a visitor comes the same day, surely the expectation so founded is not verified. The correspondence is purely fortuitous, and the reason for saying this is that when tested over a wide area of experience by concomitant variations, it is shown to have no basis in reality. It is a verbal question whether you can say that the expectation was false ; but it was certainly worthless. And to pronounce it worthless does not require you to deny that the stranger came, which it would do if the correlation were a genuine one.

With these suggestions in our minds, let us read Mr. Russell's account of a case in which a thesis is verified by consequences.

" We verify a scientific hypothesis indirectly, by deducing consequences as to the future, which subsequent experiment confirms. If somebody were to doubt whether Caesar had crossed the Rubicon, verification could only be obtained from the future.[1] We could proceed to display manuscripts to our historical sceptic, in

[1] It is instructive to ask " Future to what ? " in this passage. It must all be future to the enquirer if he has not raised the question before. But why on earth should it all be future to the event?

which it was said that Caesar had behaved
in this way.. We could advance arguments,
verifiable by future [1] experience, to prove
the antiquity of the manuscript from its
texture, colour, etc. We could find in-
scriptions agreeing with the historian on
other points, and tending to show his
general accuracy.[2] The causal laws which
our arguments would assume could be
verified by the future occurrence of events
inferred by means of them. The existence
and persistence of causal laws, it is true,
must be regarded as a fortunate accident,
and how long it will continue we cannot
tell. . . . The process is not absolute or infallible, but it has been found capable of
sifting beliefs and building up knowledge.
It affords no theoretical refutation of the
sceptic, whose position [if he holds his
tongue and refrains from action, surely,
but not otherwise] must remain logically
unassailable ; but if complete scepticism

[1] See note on preceding page.
[2] Obviously these would be equally good evidence if they
and the portion of the historian's narrative they affected were
prior to the alleged event of crossing the Rubicon.

is rejected, it gives the practical method by which the system of our beliefs grows gradually towards the unattainable ideal of impeccable knowledge."

About this description it suffices to ask a single question. If in face of the huge construction here depicted and without any new fact being brought to bear, we elect to deny that Caesar crossed the Rubicon, have we really incurred no logical liability ? Are we not in that case caught in an intolerable contradiction between our denial and the assertions which, read together in their total significance, represent the logical antecedent of which the assertion which we are denying is a consequen*t* (not temporal consequen*ce*) ? How can we deny a consequent and let the antecedent stand ? If you prefer to state the relation the other way, with more regard for time, and say the crossing is the antecedent and all the rest in its connection the consequen*ce*, yet still you cannot deny the antecedent and leave the consequence standing, in so far as the former can be shown to be the only possible antecedent from which the total consequence is inferrible.

Surely it is plain that we are affirming the crossing of the Rubicon because we cannot deny all these other matters in their connection and significance. And this *is* the method and principle of coherence, which is of course, as he says of this method, " the practical [and logical] method, by which the system of our beliefs grows gradually towards the unattainable ideal of impeccable knowledge."

Now with reference to the theory of truth we note here again that we have given up the definition by resemblance of expectation to event,[1] and have slid on to a wholly different track,[2] the track of which we had premonitions in the importance assigned to context[3] and correlation[4] for memory. We are here being told not that what is true resembles its objective, but that what is true fits into the

[1] P. 270, top.
[2] See above for the same cross-over in pp. 179, 191, 209 ff.
[3] Pp. 162-63.   [4] P. 185.

system of reality in such a way that, taking large portions of that system in connection, we find propositions connected with them which must be held on pain of abandoning those portions. To this Mr. Russell betakes himself, here as before, without turning a hair. But it is obviously a recognition of the great system of reality, dragged in to supplement the wholly inadequate and unworkable idea of truth which the description of the mind as constituted by trains of mental particulars, with a chasm between them and the objects of thought, can offer.

(δ) In the earlier part of this chapter I indicated my agreement with Mr. Russell's view of the close kinship between habit and thought. I have here only to point the moral of his attitude to what is meant by " thinking," in so far as it throws light on his reduction of mind to a complex of sensations and images. The full relation of thought to consciousness I shall deal with in a later chapter.

The thought which he admits to be real

is mainly for him identifiable with responses to stimuli, governed by habit, and including the use of language. We saw above the paradoxes in which he indulges on this subject. What looks like thought can for him, in the main, be reduced to a certain set of habits in the use of words.[1] If we add to this, what the behaviourists do not admit, the existence of images and their reproduction by association,[2] we have all that Mr. Russell understands under the term thinking. "I remain, therefore, entirely unconvinced that there is any such phenomenon as thinking which consists neither of images nor of words, or that 'ideas' have to be added to sensations and images as part of the material out of which mental phenomena are built."[3]

On the other hand, there is a great deal that is called thinking which he does not admit to be a reality, and here I should almost wholly agree with him, were it not

[1] P. 27.   [2] P. 206.
[3] P. 227. (Cf. p. 229 on knowledge of similarities and differences, which I suppose is to be construed in agreement with the above.)

that, as it seems to me, this negation has led him to suppose that in maintaining it he has dealt with the subject, and not to look for thinking anywhere else.

The first sentences of the lecture on " General Ideas and Thought " give the keynote. " It is said to be one of the merits of the human mind that it is capable of framing abstract ideas, and of conducting non-sensational thought. In this it is supposed to differ from the mind of animals. From Plato onward the ' idea ' has played a great part in the systems of leading philosophers. The 'idea' has been in their hands always something noble and abstract, the apprehension and use of which by man confers upon him a quite special dignity." And the real question is, " Seeing that there certainly are words of which the meaning is abstract, and seeing that we can use these words intelligently, what must be assumed or inferred, or what can be discovered by observation, in the way of mental content to account for the intelligent use of abstract words ? "

The main conceptions to which he is hostile, then, are the abstract general idea —general in virtue of its abstractness— and imageless thinking.[1]

As regards the first of these, I refer to the section from Lotze which I quoted on p. 81. A universal idea, he says in effect, is a problem which cannot be realised in actual mental process. The allusion to Plato of course has no bearing on the matter. Plato's forms are not mental existences at all. What we chiefly owe to Plato on the territory of theory of knowledge is the recognition of the universal as operating constructively through reproductive association—the binding together of memory and inference through a common root in the marriage of universals. I do not think there is on this head any fault, other than one of omission, to be found with Mr. Russell's account of general ideas, except that he seems to me, following Lotze and Semon, to lay too much stress on the *de facto* generality of abstract pictures,[2]

[1] Pp. 223 ff.   [2] Lotze's first universals. Cf. p. 220.

and too little on the negation, which, as
Mr. Bradley, for instance, has emphasised,[1]
is the condition necessary to the awareness
of a universal. I will return to the
omission directly.

As for imageless thought, I strongly
sympathise with Mr. Russell's observations
on Bühler's experiments. I do not venture
to deny the existence of imageless thinking; but from my earliest acquaintance
with the notion of pure thought I have
always suspected that in it extremes were
disguisedly meeting, and that what we had
before us was really a thinking which was
purely verbal. In the present case this
alternative is expressly excluded, and therefore I cannot recognise of my own experience imageless thinking at all. I believe
that in thinking there is always imagery,
partially superfluous; and that as some
of it has always to be excluded by the
negation of which we spoke in order to the
operation of the universal—the selective
element on which interest and connection

[1] *Essays*, p. 296.

hinge,—the degree of abstraction of the image has no relation to its universal character.

Nevertheless, I believe that thought, being neither sensations nor images, nor any combination of them, is the essential characteristic of mind, and that in neglecting to assign it a place in its own right, Mr. Russell has made an omission which completely mars his analysis.

Thought, I have agreed with him, is closely connected with habit; we might say that it first appears as habit, and never ceases to be akin to it. Also, I think he is right when he connects it with habit and memory as a development of mnemic causation. All this throws far more light on its nature than any identification of it with consciousness. So far, then, we are together.

What more do I want him to say? I want him to recognise that in and through the working of mnemic causation thought is the control of mental process by the real object. We find reality—Mr. Russell

III THE RUSSELL MIND 157

quite recognises this—in " whatever can
have effects upon us without our co-operation." [1] All in experience that has this
characteristic establishes itself as a unitary
world through its effect on competing
mental processes by means of inhibition,
reproductive suggestion and specification,
reinforcement by fusion—in all of which lie
the principles which ultimately emerge as
judgment and inference. The universal
operates, we have seen with Mr. Russell,
by these means within the trains of particulars which are what we light upon at
any moment in considering our mental
contents. This operation, which is the
mode by which the reality, the growing
and coherent body of experience, governs
our psychical process, is what we mean by
thought. It is this that, as we saw, refers
the image or sign of any kind to the
object—the element in the established
world—which is the meaning " of " the
sign ; and in this " of " affirms a unity
between sign and object which we noted

1 Pp. 185, 187.

in Mr. Russell's doctrine to be treated as
affirmed in expressions such as "this
occurred." These, we noted, really contain
the essence of the matter, but under the
influence of the dogmatic reduction of mind
to particulars are subsequently pronounced
not to have expressed the simple truth,
but to have resulted from a naïve confusion.

In other words, thought is the sense of
the whole, which first shows itself far down
in the organic world, where the laws of
mnemic causation are seen doing what they
can under the conditions to introduce harmony, and adaptation to the reality which
exercises power, in the primitive mind, and
later come to deal as thought with the
established unitary world, whose systematic
character, as before, they continually maintain and extend, being unable to permit
repose where any discordant mental process survives.

This is what I understand by thought ;
and obviously it does not conflict with the
view that what we light upon in our intro-

spection are always particulars. That the
particulars are always, so to speak, em-
bedded in a whole, and always, therefore,
have universals such as we experience in
habit, operating among them, guiding their
succession, and utilising them as signs—
this is the further recognition, apart from
which the theory is defective. On the
relation to consciousness of thought thus
conceived I shall have more to say later.

THE END

Printed in Great Britain by R. & R. CLARK, LIMITED, *Edinburgh.*